Great Minds

Great Companions

HERE is a book that is many things in one—a guide, a philosopher, a friend, a reference book for speakers, students, writers, teachers, a source of inspiration and of humor, and above all else, a constant joy to read and read again.

Here is the essence of civilized man's heritage—the tranquil wisdom of Thoreau, George Bernard Shaw's caustic epigram on man, Dante's thoughts on philosophy, Einstein's comment on peace, Elizabeth Barrett Browning on love, Milton's perceptive observation on fame, Michelangelo's lines on art, Plato on good government—and many, many more.

HERE are the ideas and thoughts that have helped to fashion the ways of man throughout the centuries—a distillation in one unusual, stimulating book of the most memorable and cogent lessons that great men and women have passed on to future generations. These are steadfast and eloquent companions to keep at your side. Their immortal words can be your key to a fuller, richer understanding of life—and of the intricate complexities of the human mind.

Other SIGNET KEY Books You'll Enjoy

Only 25 Cents Each

A

Treasury

OF

Wisdom and Inspiration

EDITED BY

David St. Leger

A SIGNET KEY BOOK
Published by THE NEW AMERICAN LIBRARY

Published as a SIGNET KEY BOOK
By Arrangement with Copeland & Lamm, Inc.

FIRST PRINTING, DECEMBER, 1954

ACKNOWLEDGMENTS AND COPYRIGHT NOTICES

The editor wishes to express his cordial thanks to publishers, authors, and authorized representatives, for their kind permission to reprint passages from books copyrighted or controlled by them as indicated in the following list:

GEORGE ALLEN AND UNWIN LTD.: From *A General Introduction to Psychoanalysis* (British edition, *Introductory Lectures on Psychoanalysis*) by Sigmund Freud.
BRANDT & BRANDT: From "Music I Heard With You" in *Selected Poems*, published by Charles Scribner's Sons, copyright 1919, 1921, by Conrad Aiken; from the speeches of Franklin K. Lane in *American Spirit*, copyright 1918 by Frederick A. Stokes; from "The Goose Girl" in *The Harp-Weaver and Other Poems*, published by Harper & Brothers, copyright 1921, 1949, by Edna St. Vincent Millay; from "Thursday" in *A Few Figs from Thistles*, published by Harper & Brothers, copyright 1918, 1946, by Edna St. Vincent Millay.
JOHN MASON BROWN: From *The Art of Playgoing* by John Mason Brown.
JAMES BRANCH CABELL: From *The Cream of the Jest* by James Branch Cabell, copyright 1917, 1922, 1930, 1944, by James Branch Cabell.
THE CLARENDON PRESS, Oxford: From *The Growth of Love* and *The Poetical Works*, by Robert Bridges.
GEORGE ADE DAVIS: From *Fables in Slang* by George Ade.
THE JOHN DAY COMPANY, INC.: From *The Importance of Living* by Lin Yutang, copyright 1937 by John Day Company, Inc.
J. M. DENT & SONS LTD.: From *Notes on Life and Letters* and *Under Western Eyes*, by Joseph Conrad.
DODD, MEAD & COMPANY, INC.: From "Song" in *The Collected Poems of Rupert Brooke*, Copyright 1915, by Dodd, Mead & Company, Inc.; from *The Complex Vision* by J. C. Powys, copyright 1920 by Dodd, Mead & Company, Inc.
DOUBLEDAY & COMPANY, INC.: From *The Story of My Life* by Helen Keller; from Introduction to *Poems I Remember* by John Kieran; from "Trees" in *Trees and Other Poems* by Joyce Kilmer; from "The Vampire" in *Rudyard Kipling's Verse* and "In the Neolithic Age" in *Departmental Ditties and Ballads and Barrack-Room Ballads* by Rudyard Kipling, both by permission of Mrs. George Bambridge and Doubleday & Company, Inc.; from "the wail of archy" in *Archy and Mehitabel* by Don Marquis; from *The Moon and Sixpence* by W. Somerset Maugham.

Library of Congress Catalog No. 54-7676

SIGNET KEY BOOKS are published by
The New American Library of World Literature, Inc.
501 Madison Avenue, New York 22, New York

Contents

Introduction

The wisdom of the world's famous men and women of the past and of the present is an enduring, inexhaustible source of inspiration. Great thoughts clearly, forcefully, beautifully expressed give us the very essence of the cultural heritage which has come to us enriched by the contributions of every century and every generation including our own.

In calling this new book *A Treasury of Wisdom and Inspiration,* we have indicated our feeling that in these pages every reader will find a wealth of significant, constructive, and satisfying comments and observations on life in its many aspects. Here are notable passages from the writings and sayings of outstanding thinkers and workers in every field of human endeavor. Poets, philosophers, statesmen, religious leaders, educators, business men, scientists, artists, historians—all contribute to this Treasury. The most familiar quotations included here are of perennial interest; and the less well known offer added richness, variety, and surprise.

The plan of the book makes it equally attractive for reading or browsing or reference. As shown in the Table of Contents, there are twelve main divisions, each devoted to a major topic of universal interest: Love; Spiritual Guidance; Our Country; Home and Family; Self-Improvement, Character and Personality; Literature and Art; Nature; History; Relaxation; With a Merry Heart; The World's Work; Friendship. Each of these twelve large divisions is made up of nine or ten interestingly contrasted subdivisions presenting—as their headings show—different aspects of the main theme.

Within the subdivisions, the passages of prose and verse follow one another in such a way as to enhance the interest of each. One statement in many instances reinforces the point of the preceding one; but not infrequently two adjacent statements offer striking variations of the same thought; and then quite often two passages which are almost diametrically opposed have intentionally been placed as neighbors. The reader will find that wisdom and inspiration are conveyed here not only through essential seriousness and earnestness of mood but in quite a number of instances by a lighter tone and a touch of wit.

One of our objectives has been to include a wide range of passages by prominent living and recent writers, and to have these words of today alongside the great statements of the past on similar topics. You will find here quotations from Albert Schweitzer, Sigmund Freud, Albert Einstein; from Robert Frost, Carl Sandburg, T. S. Eliot, W. H. Auden; from Ernest Hemingway, Thomas Wolfe; H. L. Mencken, John Dewey, Rachel L. Carson—to mention only a few. Their thoughts will be found on pages containing unforgettable words from the greatest sources—from the Bible; from Socrates, Plato, Aristotle, and others of ancient Greece; from Shakespeare, Milton, Walt Whitman, and the many, many other masters of prose and poetry; from the speeches and writings of the founding fathers of our country, and their successors who so nobly carried forward their work, and from those who have strengthened it to meet the needs of today.

In the Table of Contents you can readily find the topic in which you are particularly interested at a given moment. If you are eager, however, to locate the passages by a certain author or speaker, you will want to turn to the Index, which gives all names and all page references for each.

It is the editor's hope that for leisurely reading enjoyment, for briefer sampling of individual topics, and for convenient reference in preparing a talk of any sort, this new book will prove itself a welcome and handy companion and indeed a *Treasury*.

DAVID ST. LEGER

A

Treasury

OF

Wisdom and Inspiration

LOVE

The Magic of First Love

At the touch of love every one becomes a poet.

PLATO, *Symposium*

There's nothing half so sweet in life
As love's young dream.

THOMAS MOORE, *Love's Young Dream*

There is a place where love begins and a place where love ends—and love asks nothing.

CARL SANDBURG, *Explanations of Love*

The magic of first love is our ignorance that it can ever end.

BENJAMIN DISRAELI, *Henrietta Temple*

No sooner met but they looked, no sooner looked but they loved, no sooner loved but they sighed, no sooner sighed but they asked one another the reason, no sooner knew the reason but they sought the remedy.

SHAKESPEARE, *As You Like It*

It was many and many a year ago,
In a kingdom by the sea,
That a maiden there lived whom you may know
By the name of Annabel Lee;
And this maiden she lived with no other thought
Than to love and be loved by me.

EDGAR ALLAN POE, *Annabel Lee*

Love at first sight is only realizing an imagination that has always haunted us; or meeting with a face, or figure, or cast of expression in perfection that we have seen and admired in a less degree or in less favorable circumstances a hundred times before.

WILLIAM HAZLITT, *The Prose Album*

I could praise you once with beautiful words ere you came
And entered my life with love in a wind of flame.

GEORGE W. RUSSELL (AE), *The Silence of Love*

If Heaven a draught of heavenly pleasure spare,
  One cordial in this melancholy vale,
'Tis when a youthful, loving, modest pair
  In other's arms breathe out the tender tale.
        ROBERT BURNS, *The Cotter's Saturday Night*

The bashful virgin's side-long looks of love.
      OLIVER GOLDSMITH, *The Deserted Village*

One pulse of passion—youth's first fiery glow,—
Is worth the hoarded proverbs of the sage:
Vex not thy soul with dead philosophy;
Have we not lips to kiss with, hearts to love,
    and eyes to see?
          OSCAR WILDE, *Panthea*

But they were young: Oh! what without our youth
Would love be? What would youth be without love?
          BYRON, *Beppo*

It is the season now to go
About the country high and low,
Among the lilacs hand in hand,
And two by two in fairy land.
The brooding boy and sighing maid,
Wholly fain and half afraid,
Now meet along the hazel'd brook
To pass and linger, pause and look.
      ROBERT LOUIS STEVENSON, *Underwoods*

In the spring a young man's fancy lightly turns to thoughts
  of love.
        ALFRED TENNYSON, *Locksley Hall*

Love and Friendship Compared

A person once said to me that he could make nothing of love,
except that it was friendship accidentally combined with desire.
Whence I concluded that he had never been in love. For what
shall we say of the feeling which a man of sensibility has
towards his wife with her baby at her breast? How pure from
sensual desire! Yet how different from friendship!
      SAMUEL TAYLOR COLERIDGE, *Table-Talk*

Love contending with friendship, and self with each
　　generous impulse,
To and fro in his breast his thoughts were heaving
　　and dashing.

> HENRY WADSWORTH LONGFELLOW
> *The Courtship of Miles Standish*

Give all to love;
Obey thy heart;
Friends, kindred, days,
Estate, good-fame,
Plans, credit, and the Muse,—
Nothing refuse.

> RALPH WALDO EMERSON, *Give All to Love*

In love one has need of being believed, in friendship of being
understood.

> ABEL BONNARD, *The Art of Friendship*

Love is only chatter,
Friends are all that matter.

> GELETT BURGESS, *Willy and the Lady*

The feeling of friendship is like that of being comfortably
filled with roast beef; love, like being enlivened with champagne.

SAMUEL JOHNSON, (from Boswell's *Life of Samuel Johnson*)

In friendship we only see those faults which may be prejudicial
to our friends. In love we see no faults but those by which we
suffer ourselves.

> LA BRUYÈRE, *Les Caractères*

Most friendship is feigning, most loving mere folly.

> SHAKESPEARE, *As You Like It*

Nuptial love maketh mankind; friendly love perfecteth it.

> FRANCIS BACON, *Essays: Of Love*

When a Man Marries

I chose my wife, as she did her wedding gown, for qualities that would wear well.

OLIVER GOLDSMITH, *The Vicar of Wakefield*

Marriage is a very sea of calls and claims, which have but little to do with love.

HENRIK IBSEN

Two persons who have chosen each other out of all the species, with the design to be each other's mutual comfort and entertainment, have, in that action, bound themselves to be good-humored, affable, discreet, forgiving, patient, and joyful, with respect to each other's frailties and perfections, to the end of their lives.

JOSEPH ADDISON

A happy marriage is a new beginning of life, a new starting point for happiness and usefulness.

A. P. STANLEY

To have and to hold from this day forward, for better, for worse, for richer, for poorer, in sickness, and in health, to love and to cherish, till death us do part.

BOOK OF COMMON PRAYER: *Solemnization of Matrimony*

Marriage is a medicine which acts differently on good men and good women.—She does not love him quite enough—cure,—marriage.—He loves her a little too much—cure,—marriage.—

CHARLES READE

Ev'n in the happiest choice, where fav'ring heaven
Has equal love and easy fortune giv'n,—
Think not, the husband gain'd, that all is done;
The prize of happiness must still be won:
And, oft, the careless find it to their cost,
The lover in the husband may be lost;
The graces might alone his heart allure,
They and the virtues, meeting, must secure.

GEORGE LYTTELTON, *Advice to a Lady*

The only thing that can hallow marriage is love, and the only genuine marriage is that which is hallowed by love.

> Leo Tolstoy, *The Kreutzer Sonata*

Who are happy in marriage? Those with so little imagination that they cannot picture a better state, and those so shrewd that they prefer quiet slavery to hopeless rebellion.

> H. L. Mencken, *Prejudices, Series Two*

> As are those dulcet sounds in break of day
> That creep into the dreaming bridegroom's ear
> And summon him to marriage.

> Shakespeare, *The Merchant of Venice*

> She what was honour knew,
> And with obsequious majesty approv'd
> My pleaded reason. To the nuptial bow'r
> I led her blushing like the morn: all Heav'n
> And happy constellations on that hour
> Shed their selectest influence; the earth
> Gave sign of gratulation, and each hill;
> Joyous the birds; fresh gales and gentle airs
> Whisper'd it to the woods, and from their wings
> Flung rose, flung odours from the spicy shrub.

> Milton, *Paradise Lost*

> Pure, as the charities above,
> Rise the sweet sympathies of love;
> And closer chords than those of life
> Unite the husband to the wife.

> John Logan, *The Lovers*

There is, indeed, nothing that so much seduces reason from vigilance, as the thought of passing life with an amiable woman.

> Samuel Johnson, (Boswell's *Life*)

A good wife is heaven's last, best gift to man,—his gem of many virtues, his casket of jewels; her voice is sweet music, her smiles his brightest day, her kiss the guardian of his innocence, her arms the pale of his safety, her industry his surest wealth, her economy his safest steward, her lips his faithful counsellors, her bosom the softest pillow of his cares.

> Jeremy Taylor

Whatever woman may cast her lot with mine, should any ever do so, it is my intention to do all in my power to make her happy and contented; and there is nothing I can imagine that would make me more unhappy than to fail in the effort.

> ABRAHAM LINCOLN:
> Letter to *Mrs. O. H. Browning,*
> *April 1, 1838*

I want (who does not want?) a wife,
    Affectionate and fair,
To solace all the woes of life,
    And all its joys to share;
Of temper sweet, of yielding will,
    Of firm yet placid mind,
With all my faults to love me still,
    With sentiment refin'd.

> JOHN QUINCY ADAMS, *Man Wants But Little*

She is a winsome wee thing,
She is a handsome wee thing,
She is a lo'esome wee thing,
This sweet wee wife o'mine!

> BURNS, *My Wife's a Winsome Wee Thing*

Blessed is the man that hath a virtuous wife, for the number of his days shall be double. A virtuous woman rejoiceth her husband, and he shall fulfil the years of his life in peace. A good wife is a good portion.

> *Apocrypha: Ecclesiasticus,* XXVI, 1-3

The Feminine Side

But I love you, sir:
And when a woman says she loves a man,
The man must hear her, though he love her not.

> ELIZABETH BARRETT BROWNING, *Aurora Leigh*

A woman despises a man for loving her, unless she happens to return his love.

> ELIZABETH STODDARD, *Two Men*

Soft is the breath of a maiden's Yes:
Not the light gossamer stirs with less;
But never a cable that holds so fast
Through all the battles of wave and blast.
OLIVER WENDELL HOLMES, *Dorothy Q*

What country girl bewitches thy heart who knows not how to draw her dress about her ankles?

SAPPHO

Archly the maiden smiled, and, with eyes over-running
    with laughter,
Said, in a tremulous voice, "Why don't you speak for
    yourself, John?"
LONGFELLOW, *The Courtship of Miles Standish*

Men always want to be a woman's first love. That is their clumsy vanity. We women have a more subtle instinct about things. What we like is to be a man's last romance.
OSCAR WILDE, *A Woman of No Importance*

And if I loved you Wednesday,
    Well, what is that to you?
I do not love you Thursday—
    So much is true.
EDNA ST. VINCENT MILLAY, *Thursday*

A woman either loves or hates; there is no third course.
PUBLILIUS SYRUS, *Sententiae*

I loved him too as woman loves—
Reckless of sorrow, sin, or scorn.
LETITIA ELIZABETH LANDON, *The Indian Bride*

God has placed the genius of women in their hearts; because the works of this genius are always works of love.
LAMARTINE

Love preserves beauty, and the flesh of woman is fed with caresses as are bees with flowers.

ANATOLE FRANCE

We cannot fight for love, as men may do;
We should be woo'd, and were not made to woo.
SHAKESPEARE, *A Midsummer Night's Dream*

It never displeases a woman to make love to her.
CERVANTES, *Don Quixote*

Women wish to be loved without a why or a wherefore; not because they are pretty, or good, or well-bred, or graceful, or intelligent, but because they are themselves.
HENRI FRÉDÉRIC AMIEL, *Journal*

Of all the paths that lead to a woman's love
Pity's the straightest.
BEAUMONT AND FLETCHER, *The Knight of Malta*

The heart of woman tastes no truer joy,
Is never flatter'd with such dear enchantment—
'Tis more than selfish vanity—as when
She hears the praises of the man she loves.
JAMES THOMSON, *Tancred and Sigismunda*

Prithee, pretty maiden—prithee tell me true,
    (Hey, but I'm doleful, willow willow waly!)
Have you e'er a lover a dangling after you?
    Hey willow waly O!
W. S. GILBERT, *Patience*

The young girl who begins to experience the necessity of loving seeks to hide it; but the desire of pleasing betrays the secret of her heart, and sometimes reveals her hopes.
BEAUCHÊNE

The Force of Love

Ah! woe's me, that I should love and conceal;
Long have I wish'd, but never dare reveal,
Even though severely love's pains I feel;
Xerxes that great, was't free from Cupid's dart,
And all the greatest heroes felt the smart.
GEORGE WASHINGTON
(from an untitled poem written before 1748)

Love has a tide.

HELEN HUNT

Love supreme defies all sophistry.

GEORGE ELIOT

Love is precisely to the moral nature what the sun is to the earth.

BALZAC

Riches take wings, comforts vanish, hope withers away, but love stays with us. Love is God.

LEW WALLACE

No cord or cable can draw so forcibly, or bind so fast, as love can do with only a single thread.

BURTON

Love is the beginning, the middle, and the end of everything.

LACORDAIRE

O love, resistless in thy might, thou triumphest
even over gold!

SOPHOCLES, *Antigone*

Were beauty under twenty locks kept fast,
Yet love breaks through and picks them all at last.

SHAKESPEARE, *Venus and Adonis*

I have found it impossible to carry the heavy burden of responsibility and to discharge my duties as king as I would wish to do without the help and support of the woman I love.

EDWARD VIII, *Radio broadcast, December 11, 1936*

This Emotion's Essence

A pity beyond all telling.
Is hid in the heart of love.

WILLIAM BUTLER YEATS, *The Pity of Love*

Now Love masters my limbs and shakes me, fatal creature, bittersweet.

SAPPHO

Love is fostered by confidence and constancy; he who is able to give much is able also to love much.

PROPERTIUS, *Elegies*

Love's mysteries in souls do grow
But yet the body is his book.

JOHN DONNE, *The Ecstasy*

Oh, how this Spring of love resembleth
Th' uncertain glory of an April day,
Which now shows all the beauty of the sun,
And by and by a cloud takes all away.

SHAKESPEARE, *Two Gentlemen of Verona*

Love and smoke are two things which can't be concealed.

FRENCH PROVERB

Love withers under constraint: its very essence is liberty: it is compatible neither with obedience, jealousy, nor fear: it is there most pure, perfect, and unlimited where its votaries live in confidence, equality, and unreserve.

PERCY BYSSHE SHELLEY, *Fragment*

Ask not of me, love, what is love?
Ask what is good of God above—
Ask of the great sun what is light—
Ask what is darkness of the night—
Ask sin of what may be forgiven—
Ask what is happiness of Heaven—
Ask what is folly of the crowd—
Ask what is fashion of the shroud—
Ask what is sweetness of thy kiss—
Ask of thyself what beauty is.

P. J. BAILEY, *Festus*

Love, as is told by the seers of old,
Comes as a butterfly tipped with gold,
    Flutters and flies in sunlit skies,
Weaving round hearts that were one time cold.
                ALGERNON CHARLES SWINBURNE, *Song*

"Oh! Love," they said, "is King of Kings,
    And Triumph is his crown.
Earth fades in flame before his wings,
    And Sun and Moon bow down."
                RUPERT BROOKE, *Song*

I could not love thee, Dear, so much
    Loved I not Honour more.
RICHARD LOVELACE, *To Lucasta on Going to the Wars*

Love! the surviving gift of Heaven,
    The choicest sweet of paradise,
    In life's else bitter cup distilled.
    THOMAS CAMPBELL, *Ode to the Memory of Burns*

Love is God's essence; Power but his attribute: therefore is
his love greater than his power.
            RICHARD GARNETT, *De Flagello Myrteo*

True love's the gift which God has given
To man alone beneath the heaven;
It is the secret sympathy,
The silver link, the silken tie,
Which heart to heart, and mind to mind,
In body and in soul can bind.
          SIR WALTER SCOTT, *Lay of the Last Minstrel*

But love is such a mystery
    I cannot find it out:
For when I think I'm best resolved,
    I then am most in doubt.
          SIR JOHN SUCKLING, *Song: I Prithee*
          Send Me Back My Heart

Male and Female

Oh! a man's love is strong
    When fain he comes a-mating.
But a woman's love is long
    And grows when it is waiting.
                LAURENCE HOUSMAN, *The Two Loves*

Love is so different with us men.
                ROBERT BROWNING, *In a Year*

To a man the disappointment of love may occasion some
bitter pangs: it wounds some feelings of tenderness—it blasts
some prospects of felicity; but he is an active being—he may
dissipate his thoughts in the whirl of varied occupation. But
woman's is comparatively a fixed, a secluded, and meditative
life. She is more the companion of her own thoughts and
feelings. Her lot is to be wooed and won; and if unhappy in
her love, her heart is like some fortress that has been captured,
and sacked, and abandoned, and left desolate.
                WASHINGTON IRVING, *The Sketch Book*

Love, that of every woman's heart
Will have the whole, and not a part,
That is to her, in Nature's plan,
More than ambition is to man,
Her light, her life, her very breath,
With no alternative but death.
                LONGFELLOW, *The Golden Legend*

Love lessens woman's delicacy and increases man's.
                JEAN PAUL RICHTER

I know a woman's portion when she loves,
It's hers to give, my darling, not to take;
It isn't lockets, dear, nor pairs of gloves,
It isn't marriage bells nor wedding cake,
It's up and cook, although the belly ache;
And bear the child, and up and work again,
And count a sick man's grumble worth the pain.
                JOHN MASEFIELD, *The Widow in the Bye Street*

Man's love is of man's life a thing apart,
'Tis woman's whole existence: man may range
The court, camp, church, the vessel, and the mart,
Sword, gown, gain, glory, offer in exchange
Pride, fame, ambition, to fill up his heart,
And few there are whom these cannot estrange;
Men have all these resources, we but one,
To love again, and be again undone.

BYRON, *Don Juan*

Love, which is only an episode in the life of man, is the entire history of woman's life.

MADAME DE STAËL

Wooers and Wooing

O gentle Romeo,
If thou dost love, pronounce it faithfully.
Or if thou think'st I am too quickly won,
I'll frown and be perverse and say thee nay,
So thou wilt woo.

SHAKESPEARE, *Romeo and Juliet*

Come live with me and be my Love
And we will all the pleasures prove.

CHRISTOPHER MARLOWE, *The Passionate Shepherd*

"When a man says he's willin'," said Mr. Barkis, "it's as much as to say, that man's a-waitin' for a answer."

DICKENS, *David Copperfield*

Much ado there was, God wot!
He would love and she would not.
She said, Never was man true;
He said, None was false to you.
He said, He had lov'd her long;
She said, Love should have no wrong.
Coridon would kiss her then;
She said, Maids must kiss no men
Till they did for good and all.

NICHOLAS BRETON, *Phillida and Coridon*

He that would the daughter win,
Must with the mother first begin.
                    JOHN RAY, *English Proverbs*

When words we want, love teacheth to indite,
And what we blush to speak she bids us write.
          WILLIAM MATHER, *The Young Man's Companion*

A fool there was and he made his prayer
        (Even as you and I!)
To a rag and a bone and a hank of hair
        (We called her the woman who did not care)
But the fool he called her his lady fair—
        (Even as you and I!)
                    RUDYARD KIPLING, *The Vampire*

Kissing Plus

A kiss, when all is said, what is it?
A rosy dot placed on the "i" in loving;
'Tis a secret told to the mouth instead of to the ear.
              EDMOND ROSTAND, *Cyrano de Bergerac*

Stolen kisses are always sweeter.
                    LEIGH HUNT, *The Indicator*

"May I print a kiss on your lips?" I said,
    And she nodded her full permission;
So we went to press and I rather guess
    We printed a full edition.
              JOSEPH LILIENTHAL, *A Full Edition*

Tell me who first did kisses suggest?
It was a mouth all glowing and blest;
It kissed and it thought of nothing beside.
                  HEINRICH HEINE, *Book of Songs*

All the breath and the bloom of the year in the bag
        of one bee:
    All the wonder and wealth of the mine in the heart
        of one gem:

In the core of one pearl all the shade and the shine
        of the sea:
Breath and bloom, shade and shine—wonder, wealth, and—
        how far above them—
                Truth, that's brighter than gem,
                Trust, that's purer than pearl—
Brightest truth, purest trust in the universe—
        all were for me
                In the kiss of one girl.
                        ROBERT BROWNING, *Summum Bonum*

You kissed me! My head dropped low on your breast
With a feeling of shelter and infinite rest,
While the holy emotions my tongue dared not speak
Flashed up as a flame from my heart to my cheek.
            JOSEPHINE SLOCUM HUNT, *You Kissed Me*

She kissed his brow, his cheek, his chin,
And where she ends she doth anew begin.
            SHAKESPEARE, *Venus and Adonis*

Lovers live by love as larks live by leeks.
            JOHN HEYWOOD, *Proverbs*

The wine of Love is music,
        And the feast of Love is song:
And when Love sits down to the banquet,
        Love sits long:
Sits long and rises drunken,
        But not with the feast and the wine;
He reeleth with his own heart,
        That great, rich Vine.
                    JAMES THOMSON, *The Vine*

There is no sorrow like a love denied
Nor any joy like love that has its will.
        RICHARD HOVEY, *The Marriage of Guenevere*

Anthea bade me tie her shoe;
I did, and kissed the instep too;
And would have kissed unto her knee,
Had not her blush rebuked me.
                    ROBERT HERRICK, *Hesperides*

After kissing comes more kindness.

JOHN CLARKE, *Parœmiologia Anglo-Latina*

Come, my Celia, let us prove,
While we can, the sports of love.
Time will not be ours forever,
He, at length, our good will sever.

BEN JONSON, *Volpone*

Three Little Words

If yet I have not all thy love
Dear, I shall never have it all.

JOHN DONNE, *Love's Infiniteness*

Talking of love is making it.

JOHN RAY, *English Proverbs*

You have ravish'd me away by a Power I cannot resist; and yet
I could resist till I saw you; and even since I have seen you
I have endeavored often "to reason against the reasons of my
Love."

KEATS, *(from a letter to Fanny Brawne)*

Except I be by Silvia in the night,
There is no music in the nightingale;
Unless I look on Silvia in the day,
There is no day for me to look upon.

SHAKESPEARE, *The Two Gentlemen of Verona*

Shall I, wasting in despair,
Die because a woman's fair?

GEORGE WITHER, *The Manly Heart*

Daisy, Daisy, give me your answer, do!
I'm half crazy all for the love of you!
It won't be a stylish marriage,
I can't afford a carriage,
But you'll look sweet upon the seat
Of a bicycle built for two.

HARRY DACRE, *Daisy Bell*, 1892

I loved you ere I knew you; know you now,
And having known you, love you better still.
OWEN MEREDITH, *Vanini*

I love thee, I love but thee,
With a love that shall not die
    Till the sun grows cold,
    And the stars are old,
And the leaves of the Judgment Book unfold!
BAYARD TAYLOR, *Bedouin Song*

Will you love me in December as you do in May,
Will you love me in the good old fashioned way?
    When my hair has all turned gray,
    Will you kiss me then and say,
That you love me in December as you do in May?
JAMES J. WALKER, *Will You Love Me
in December as You Do in May?*

SPIRITUAL GUIDANCE

In Praise of the Bible

I believe the Bible is the best gift God has ever given to man. All the good from the Saviour of the world is communicated to us through this book.

ABRAHAM LINCOLN

The Bible is worth all other books which have ever been printed.

PATRICK HENRY

You will find the eternal verities in the eternal Book—*and only there*. The Bible is the record of God's dealings with men, humble men for the most part, men with problems that kept them awake nights, men with doubts that ate into their hearts. The Bible shows what happens when God touches a man, a single individual.

DANIEL A. POLING, *Courage and Confidence from the Bible*

If there is anything in my thoughts or style to commend, the credit is due to my parents for instilling in me an early love of the Scriptures. If we abide by the principles taught in the Bible, our country will go on prospering and to prosper; but if we and our posterity neglect its instructions and authority, no man can tell how sudden a catastrophe may overwhelm us and bury all our glory in profound obscurity.

DANIEL WEBSTER

The Bible is the sheet-anchor of our liberties.

ULYSSES S. GRANT

The Bible is the truest utterance that ever came by alphabetic letters from the soul of man, through which, as through a window divinely opened, all men can look into the stillness of eternity, and discern in glimpses their far-distant, long-forgotten home.

THOMAS CARLYLE

The grand old Book still stands; and this old earth, the more its leaves are turned over and pondered, the more it will sustain and illustrate the pages of the Sacred Word.

CHARLES A. DANA

It is a plain old Book, modest as nature itself, and as simple, too; a book of an unpretending work-day appearance, like the sun that warms or the bread that nourishes us. And the name of this book is simply—the Bible.

HEINRICH HEINE

The whole hope of human progress is suspended on the ever growing influence of the Bible.

W. H. SEWARD

That book, sir, is the rock on which our republic rests.

ANDREW JACKSON

In all my perplexities and distresses, the Bible has never failed to give me light and strength.

ROBERT E. LEE

So great is my veneration for the Bible that the earlier my children begin to read it the more confident will be my hope that they will prove useful citizens of their country and respectable members of society. I have for many years made it a practice to read through the Bible once every year.

JOHN QUINCY ADAMS

It is impossible to enslave mentally or socially a Bible-reading people. The principles of the Bible are the ground-work of human freedom.

HORACE GREELEY

All human discoveries seem to be made only for the purpose of confirming more and more strongly the truths contained in the Sacred Scriptures.

SIR WILLIAM HERSCHEL

Bible reading is an education in itself.

TENNYSON

The Bible is literature, not dogma.

GEORGE SANTAYANA

The Bible has been the Magna Charta of the poor and oppressed. The human race is not in a position to dispense with it.

THOMAS HENRY HUXLEY

The New Testament is the very best book that ever was or ever will be known in the world.

CHARLES DICKENS

Let mental culture go on advancing, let the natural sciences progress in ever greater extent and depth, and the human mind widen itself as much as it desires; beyond the elevation and moral culture of Christianity, as it shines forth in the Gospels, it will not go.

GOETHE

Born in the East and clothed in Oriental form and imagery, the Bible walks the ways of all the world with familiar feet and enters land after land to find its own everywhere. It has learned to speak in hundreds of languages to the heart of man. Children listen to its stories with wonder and delight, and wise men ponder them as parables of life.

HENRY VAN DYKE

> We search the world for truth; we cull
> The good, the pure, the beautiful,
> From graven stone and written scroll,
> From all old flower-fields of the soul;
> And, weary seekers of the best,
> We come back laden from our quest,
> To find that all the sages said
> Is in the Book our mothers read.

JOHN GREENLEAF WHITTIER

The Meaning of Religion

Great is truth, and it prevaileth.
Bible, Vulgate Edition, III Esdras, IV, 41

The place where men meet to seek the highest is holy ground.

FELIX ADLER

> Each cloud-capped mountain is a holy altar;
> An organ breathes in every grove;
> And the full heart's a Psalter,
> Rich in deep hymns of gratitude and love.

THOMAS HOOD, *Ode to Rae Wilson*

When religion is banished, human authority totters to its fall.

POPE BENEDICT XV

The most beautiful and most profound emotion we can experience is the sensation of the mystical. It is the power of all true science . . . To know that what is impenetrable to us really exists, manifesting itself as the highest wisdom and the most radiant beauty which our dull faculties can comprehend only in their most primitive forms—this knowledge, this feeling, is at the center of true religiousness.

ALBERT EINSTEIN

Religion is life, philosophy is thought; religion looks up, friendship looks in. We need both thought and life, and we need that the two shall be in harmony.

JAMES FREEMAN CLARKE, *Ten Great Religions*

Whoso fighteth for the religion of God, whether he be slain or be victorious, we will give him a great reward.

The Koran

One religion is as true as another.

ROBERT BURTON, *Anatomy of Melancholy*

The highest flights of charity, devotion, trust, patience, bravery to which the wings of human nature have spread themselves have been flown for religious ideals.

WILLIAM JAMES, *Varieties of Religious Experience*

Each is not for its own sake,
I say the whole earth and all the stars in the
    sky are for religion's sake.
I say no man has ever yet been half devout enough,
None has ever yet adored or worship'd half enough,
None has begun to think how divine he himself is,
    and how certain the future is.
I say that the real and permanent grandeur of
    these States must be their religion.

WALT WHITMAN, *Starting from Paumanok*

I would no more quarrel with a man because of his religion than I would because of his art.

MARY BAKER EDDY, *Miscellany*

I see that sensible men and conscientious men all over the world were of one religion,—the religion of well-doing and daring.

RALPH WALDO EMERSON, *Lectures and Biographical Sketches*

Religions are opposed to one another in their form, in the material details of the cult, and in the human interpretations of symbols. They all agree on the existence of God, on the virtues, and on moral rules. Purity, goodness, beauty, faith are venerated everywhere, and it is they which should rule.

LECOMTE DU NOÜY, *Human Destiny*

Our ideal is seeking us. Open your eyes, it is here, in your home, in the multitudinous acts of mutual love and sacrifice, in the exalted experience of friendship, in shop, store and office, in your community, in social work, in civic work, in religious work, in the humblest and highest task it is there.

RABBI ABBA HILLEL SILVER, *from a sermon, "The Vision Splendid"*

Every religion is good that teaches man to be good.

THOMAS PAINE, *Rights of Man*

There is only one religion, though there are a hundred versions of it.

GEORGE BERNARD SHAW, *Plays Pleasant and Unpleasant*

American fair play would guarantee to every man the right to worship God according to his own convictions and not according to the persuasions or prejudices of his neighbor.

RABBI STEPHEN S. WISE

Religion! What treasure untold
    Resides in that heavenly word!
More precious than silver and gold,
    Or all that this earth can afford.

WILLIAM COWPER, *Verses Supposed to be Written by Alexander Selkirk*

The Power of Prayer

Prayer moves the Hand which moves the world.
JOHN AIKMAN WALLACE, *There Is an
Eye That Never Sleeps*

Prayer is a powerful thing; for God has bound and tied himself thereunto.

MARTIN LUTHER

Who rises from Prayer a better man, his prayer is answered.
GEORGE MEREDITH, *The Ordeal of Richard Feverel*

The prayer of faith shall save the sick.
New Testament: James, v, 15

The highest prayer is not one of faith merely; it is demonstration. Such prayer heals sickness, and must destroy sin and death.

MARY BAKER EDDY, *Science and Health*

Whosoever shall say unto this mountain, Be thou removed and be thou cast into the sea; and shall not doubt in his heart, but shall believe that those things which he saith shall come to pass; he shall have whatsoever he saith. Therefore I say unto you, What things soever ye desire, when ye pray, believe that ye receive them, and ye shall receive them.
New Testament: Mark, XI, 23, 24

More things are wrought by prayer
Than this world dreams of.
TENNYSON, *Morte d'Arthur*

Time spent on the knees in prayer will do more to remedy heart strain and nerve worry than anything else.
GEORGE DAVID STEWART, *from a lecture
at New York University*

The Lord's Prayer contains the sum total of religion and morals.

DUKE OF WELLINGTON

Do you wish to find out the really sublime? Repeat the Lord's Prayer.

NAPOLEON

O, do not pray for easy lives. Pray to be stronger men. Do not pray for tasks equal to your powers. Pray for powers equal to your tasks.

PHILLIPS BROOKS, *Going Up to Jerusalem*

My words fly up, my thoughts remain below:
Words without thoughts never to heaven go.

SHAKESPEARE, *Hamlet*

The day returns and brings us the petty round of irritating concerns and duties. Help us to play the man, help us to perform them with laughter and kind faces; let cheerfulness abound with industry. Give us to go blithely on our business all this day, bring us to our resting beds weary and content and undishonored, and grant us in the end the gift of sleep.

ROBERT LOUIS STEVENSON, *Prayer*

Man's Unconquerable Soul

Out of the night that covers me,
    Black as the pit from pole to pole,
I thank whatever gods may be
    For my unconquerable soul.

WILLIAM ERNEST HENLEY, *Invictus*

God created man to be immortal, and made him to be an image of his own eternity.

Apocrypha: Wisdom of Solomon, II, 23

If I err in my belief that the souls of men are immortal, I err gladly, and I do not wish to lose so delightful an error.

CICERO, *De Senectute*

Though inland far we be
Our souls have sight of that immortal sea
Which brought us hither.

WILLIAM WORDSWORTH, *Ode on the Intimations of Immortality*

I swear I think now that every thing without exception has
an eternal soul!
The trees have, rooted in the ground; the weeds of the sea
have! the animals!

WALT WHITMAN, *Leaves of Grass*

I am a better believer, and all serious souls are better believers,
in immortality than we can give grounds for.

EMERSON, *Immortality*

I believe in the immortality of the soul, not in the sense in
which I accept the demonstrable truths of science, but as a
supreme act of faith in the reasonableness of God's work.

JOHN FISKE, *The Destiny of Man*

The intellect of man sits visibly enthroned upon his forehead
and in his eye, and the heart of man is written upon his
countenance. But the soul reveals itself in the voice only, as
God revealed Himself to the prophet of old in the still small
voice, and in the voice from the burning bush.

LONGFELLOW

I am fully convinced that the soul is indestructible, and that
its activity will continue through eternity. It is like the sun,
which, to our eyes, seems to set in night; but it has in reality
only gone to diffuse its light elsewhere.

GOETHE

Whether or not the philosophers care to admit that we have
a soul, it seems obvious that we are equipped with something
or other which generates dreams and ideals, and which sets up
values.

JOHN ERSKINE

The human soul is a silent harp in God's quire, whose strings
need only to be swept by the divine breath to chime in with
the harmonies of creation.

HENRY DAVID THOREAU, *Journal*

For what is a man profited if he shall gain the whole world
and lose his own soul? or what shall a man give in exchange
for his soul?

New Testament: Matthew, XVI, 26

Star to star vibrates light; may soul to soul
Strike thro' a finer element of her own?
                    TENNYSON, *Aylmer's Field*

Be careless in your dress if you must, but keep a tidy soul.
                    MARK TWAIN, *Pudd'nhead Wilson's Calendar*

Build thee more stately mansions, O my soul,
        As the swift seasons roll!
        Leave thy low-vaulted past!
Let each new temple, nobler than the last,
Shut thee from heaven with a dome more vast,
        Till thou at length are free,
Leaving thine outgrown shell by life's unresting sea!
        OLIVER WENDELL HOLMES, *The Chambered Nautilus*

        A charge to keep I have,
            A God to glorify:
        A never-dying soul to save,
            And fit it for the sky.
                CHARLES WESLEY, *Christian Fidelity*

    Give thanks, O heart, for the high souls
    That point us to the deathless goals:
    Brave souls that took the perilous trail
    And felt the vision could not fail.
            EDWIN MARKHAM, *Conscripts of the Dream*

        Yet stab at thee that will,
        No stab the soul can kill!
            SIR WALTER RALEIGH, *The Lie*

    Life, like a dome of many-colored glass,
    Stains the white radiance of Eternity.
            PERCY BYSSHE SHELLEY, *Adonais*

The dust's for crawling, heaven's for flying,
Wherefore, O Soul, whose wings are grown,
Soar upward to the sun!
        EDGAR LEE MASTERS, *The Spoon River Anthology*

Grace of Spirit

Grace has been defined, the outward expression of the inward harmony of the soul.

WILLIAM HAZLITT

My grace is sufficient for thee: for my strength is made perfect in weakness.

New Testament: II Corinthians, XII, 9

So grace is a gift of God and kind wit a chance.

WILLIAM LANGLAND, *Piers Plowman*

From vulgar bounds with brave disorder part,
And snatch a grace beyond the reach of Art.

ALEXANDER POPE, *An Essay on Criticism*

It is the spiritual always which determines the material.

THOMAS CARLYLE, *Heroes and Hero-Worship*

More brightly must my spirit shine
Since grace of beauty is not mine.

JANIE SCREVEN HEYWARD, *The Spirit's Grace*

Spirits are not finely touch'd
But to fine issues.

SHAKESPEARE, *Measure for Measure*

The life of any one can by no means be changed after death; an evil life can in no wise be converted into a good life, or an infernal into an angelic life: because every spirit, from head to foot, is of the character of his love, and therefore, of his life; and to convert this life into its opposite, would be to destroy the spirit utterly.

SWEDENBORG, *Heaven and Hell*

True grace is natural, not artificial, because, however strenuously you strive to gain it, when it is gained it never gives the impression of effort or straining for effect.

F. D. HUNTINGTON

An inborn grace that nothing lacked
Of culture or appliance—
The warmth of genial courtesy,
The calm of self-reliance.

JOHN GREENLEAF WHITTIER

Not by matted locks, nor by lineage, nor by caste is one a Brahmin; he is the Brahmin in whom are truth and righteousness and purity.

GAUTAMA BUDDHA, *Dhammapada*

And Friends everywhere, meet together, . . . and watch over one another in that which is Eternal, and see every one, that your words be from the Eternal Life . . . And all meet together everywhere, and in your meetings wait upon the Lord, and take heed of forming words, but mind the Power, and know that which is Eternal, which will keep you all in Unity, walking in the Spirit, and will let you see the Lord near you and amongst you.

GEORGE FOX, *A Day-Book of Counsel and Comfort*

There is no substitute for the new spirit and the new way of life. We shall need experts, wise guides, persons who have clear insight and sound wisdom, but with experts or no experts, we shall never get our happy, joyous, peaceful world until we learn to love and understand and share and become brothers to one another, because we are children of a common Father. The cultivation and practice of this spirit are essential features of Quakerism.

RUFUS M. JONES, *The Quakers' Faith and Practice*

The Hand of Providence

Providence cares for every hungry mouth.

ROBERT BROWNING, *Ferishtah's Fancies*

God never sendeth mouth but he sendeth meat.

JOHN HEYWOOD, *Proverbs*

What in me is dark,
Illumine; what is low, raise and support;
That to the height of this great argument
I may assert eternal Providence,
And justify the ways of God to men.

MILTON, *Paradise Lost*

He that doth the ravens feed,
Yea, providently caters for the sparrow,
Be comfort to my age!

SHAKESPEARE, *As You Like It*

Judge not the Lord by feeble sense,
But trust Him for His grace;
Behind a frowning Providence
He hides a smiling face.

WILLIAM COWPER, *Light Shining Out of Darkness*

To the dim and bewildered vision of humanity, God's care is
more evident in some instances than in others; and upon such
instances men seize, and call them providences. It is well that
they can; but it would be gloriously better if they could believe
that the whole matter is one grand providence.

GEORGE MACDONALD

Everything that happens in the world is part of a great plan
of God, running through all time.

HENRY WARD BEECHER

By going a few minutes sooner or later, by stopping to speak
with a friend on the corner, by meeting this man or that, or by
turning down this street instead of the other, we may let slip
some impending evil, by which the whole current of our lives
would have been changed. There is no possible solution in the
dark enigma but the one word, "Providence".

LONGFELLOW

I cannot believe that God plays dice with the Cosmos.

ALBERT EINSTEIN

Who finds not Providence all good and wise,
Alike in what it gives and what it denies?

POPE, *Essay on Man*

He who is truly religious finds a providence not more truly in the history of the world than in his own personal and family history.—The rainbow which hangs a splendid circle in the heights of heaven, is also formed by the same sun in the dewdrop of the lowly flower.

JEAN PAUL RICHTER

A sense sublime
Of something far more deeply interfused,
Whose dwelling is the light of setting suns,
And the round ocean, and the living air,
And the blue sky, and in the mind of man.

WILLIAM WORDSWORTH,
Lines Composed a Few Miles above Tintern Abbey

The providence that watches over the affairs of men, works out of their mistakes, at times, a healthier issue than could have been accomplished by their own wisest forethought.

JAMES ANTHONY FROUDE

To see a world in a grain of sand,
And a heaven in a wild flower,
Hold infinity in the palm of your hand,
And eternity in an hour.

WILLIAM BLAKE, *Auguries of Innocence*

What is the operation we call Providence? There lies the unspoken thing, present, omnipresent. Every time we converse we translate it into speech.

EMERSON, *Essays*

He maketh kings to sit in soveraity;
He maketh subjects to their power obey;
He pulleth down, he setteth up on high;
He gives to this, from that he takes away;
For all we have is his: what he list do he may.

EDMUND SPENSER, *Faerie Queene*

Behind the dim unknown,
Standeth God within the shadow, keeping
watch above his own.

LOWELL, *The Present Crisis*

Fullness of Faith

Faith is the substance of things hoped for, the evidence of things not seen.

New Testament: Hebrews, XI, 1

And we shall be made truly wise if we be made content; content, too, not only with what we can understand, but content with what we do not understand—the habit of mind which theologians call—and rightly—faith in God.

CHARLES KINGSLEY, *Health and Education: On Bio-Geology*

The only faith that wears well and holds its color in all weathers is that which is woven of conviction and set with the sharp mordant of experience.

LOWELL, *My Study Windows: Abraham Lincoln*

> Wake in our breast the living fires,
> The holy faith that warmed our sires.
> OLIVER WENDELL HOLMES, *Army Hymn*

A perfect faith would lift us absolutely above fear.

GEORGE MACDONALD, *Sir Gibbie*

> Strong Son of God, immortal Love,
> Whom we, that have not seen thy face,
> By faith, and faith alone, embrace,
> Believing where we cannot prove.
> TENNYSON, *In Memoriam*

The mason asks but a narrow shelf to spring his brick from; man requires only an infinitely narrower one to spring his arch of faith from.

THOREAU, *Journal*

> We live by Faith; but Faith is not the slave
> Of text and legend. Reason's voice and God's,
> Nature's and Duty's, never are at odds.
> WHITTIER, *Requirement*

I believe in God as I believe in my friends, because I feel the breath of His affection, feel His invisible and intangible hand, drawing me, leading me, grasping me; because I possess an inner consciousness of a particular providence and of a universal mind that marks out for me the course of my own destiny.

MIGUEL DE UNAMUNO, *The Tragic Sense of Life*

The disease with which the human mind now labors is want of faith.

EMERSON, *Essays*

We walk by faith, not by sight.

New Testament: II Corinthians, v, 7

Faith is kept alive in us, and gathers strength, more from practice than from speculations.

JOSEPH ADDISON, *The Spectator*

No man has power to let another prescribe his faith. Faith is not faith without believing.

THOMAS JEFFERSON, *Notes on Religion*

Strong beliefs win strong men, and then make them stronger.

WALTER BAGEHOT, *Physics and Politics*

No iron chain, or outward force of any kind, could ever compel the soul of man to believe or to disbelieve.

THOMAS CARLYLE, *Heroes and Hero-Worship*

Fields are won by those who believe in the winning.

T. W. HIGGINSON, *Americanism in Literature*

Lord, I believe; help thou mine unbelief.

New Testament: Mark, IX, 24

I have believed the best of every man,
And find that to believe it is enough
To make a bad man show him at his best,
Or even a good man swing his lantern higher.

WILLIAM BUTLER YEATS, *Deirdre*

He does not believe that does not live according to his belief.
THOMAS FULLER, Gnomologia

> One in whom persuasion and belief
> Had ripened into faith, and faith become
> A passionate intuition.
WORDSWORTH, The Excursion

Hope Springs Eternal

The natural flights of the human mind are not from pleasure to pleasure, but from hope to hope.
SAMUEL JOHNSON, The Rambler

My hopes are not always realized, but I always hope.
OVID, Heroides

Hope to the end.
New Testament: I Peter, I, 13

> Hope springs eternal in the human breast:
> Man never is, but always to be, blest.
> The soul, uneasy and confin'd from home,
> Rests and expatiates in a life to come.
POPE, Essay on Man

While there's life, there's hope.
CICERO, Epistolæ ad Atticum

> Stone walls do not a prison make
> Nor iron bars a cage.
RICHARD LOVELACE, To Althea from Prison

Ere now I would have ended my miseries in death, but fond Hope keeps the spark alive, whispering ever that tomorrow will be better than today.
TIBULLUS, Elegies

> I live on hope and that I think do all
> Who come into this world.
ROBERT BRIDGES, Sonnets

Hope and patience are two sovereign remedies for all, the surest reposals, the softest cushions to lean on in adversity.

ROBERT BURTON, *Anatomy of Melancholy*

'Tis hope supports each noble flame,
    'Tis hope inspires poetic lays;
Our heroes fight in hopes of fame,
    And poets write in hopes of praise.
She sings sweet songs of future years,
    And dries the tears of present sorrow;
Bids doubting mortals cease their fears,
    And tells them of a bright to-morrow.

JEFFERSON, *To Ellen,* (from his *Literary Bible*)

Behind the cloud the starlight lurks,
    Through showers the sunbeams fall;
For God, who loveth all His works,
    Has left His hope with all!

WHITTIER, *A Dream of Summer*

Our greatest good, and what we least can spare,
Is hope; the last of all our evils, fear.

JOHN ARMSTRONG, *Art of Preserving Health*

Work without Hope draws nectar in a sieve,
And Hope without an object cannot live.

COLERIDGE, *Work Without Hope*

Tomorrow to fresh woods, and pastures new.

JOHN MILTON, *Lycidas*

Something will turn up.

BENJAMIN DISRAELI, *Popanilla*

Strength Through Goodness

Strengthen me by sympathizing with my strength not my weakness.

AMOS BRONSON ALCOTT, *Table-Talk: Sympathy*

Success to the strongest, who are always, at last, the wisest and best.

> RALPH WALDO EMERSON, *Uncollected Lectures:*
> *Public and Private Education*

It is not strength, but art, obtains the prize,
And to be swift is less than to be wise.

> HOMER, *Iliad* (Pope transl.)

They that wait upon the Lord shall renew their strength.

> *Old Testament: Isaiah*, XL, 31

True goodness springs from a man's own heart. All men are born good.

> CONFUCIUS, *Analects*

The good, as I conceive it, is happiness, happiness for each man after his own heart, and for each hour according to its inspiration.

> GEORGE SANTAYANA, *Soliloquies in England*

It's guid to be merry and wise,
It's guid to be honest and true.

> ROBERT BURNS, *Here's a Health to Them That's Awa*

Goodness does not more certainly make men happy than happiness makes them good.

> W. S. LANDOR, *Imaginary Conversations:*
> *Lord Brooke and Sir Philip Sidney*

You are not only good yourself, but the cause of goodness in others.

> SOCRATES, to Protagoras, (from Plato, *Protagoras*)

Good, the more
Communicated, more abundant grows.

> JOHN MILTON, *Paradise Lost*

As good people's very scarce, what I says is, make the most on 'em.

> CHARLES DICKENS, *Sketches by Boz*

Were a star quenched on high,
    For ages would its light,
Still travelling downward from the sky,
    Shine on our mortal sight.
So when a great man dies,
    For years beyond our ken,
The light he leaves behind him lies
    Upon the paths of men.
              LONGFELLOW, *Charles Sumner*

No evil can happen to a good man, either in life or after death.
        SOCRATES (from Plato, *Apology of Socrates*)

Roaming in thought over the Universe, I saw the little that
    is Good steadily hastening towards immortality,
And the vast all that is call'd Evil I saw hastening to merge
    itself and become lost and dead.
              WALT WHITMAN, *Leaves of Grass*

I live for those who love me,
    For those who know me true;
For the Heaven that smiles above me,
    And awaits my spirit too;
For the cause that lacks assistance,
For the wrong that needs resistance,
For the future in the distance,
    And the good that I can do.
          G. LINNÆUS BANKS, *What I Live For*

The mind is its own place, and in itself
Can make a Heaven of Hell, a Hell of Heaven.
          JOHN MILTON, *Paradise Lost*

In goodness there are all kinds of wisdom.
          EURIPIDES, *Alcestis*

Be good yourself and the world will be good.
          HINDU Proverb

God in Our Life

God is love; and he that dwelleth in love dwelleth in God, and God in him.
New Testament: I John, IV, 16

God is the one great employer, thinker, planner, supervisor.
HENRY WARD BEECHER

From thee, great God, we spring; to thee we tend;
Path, motive, guide, original, and end.
SAMUEL JOHNSON, *The Rambler*

God shall be my hope,
My stay, my guide and lantern to my feet.
SHAKESPEARE, *II Henry VI*

In the faces of men and women I see God
WALT WHITMAN, *Song of Myself*

Our lives are merely strange dark interludes in the electrical display of God the Father!
EUGENE O'NEILL, *Strange Interlude*

God enters by a private door into every individual.
EMERSON, *Essays*

Whate'er we leave to God, God does
And blesses us.
THOREAU, *Inspiration*

We, in some unknown Power's employ,
Move on a rigorous line:
Can neither, when we will, enjoy,
Nor, when we will, resign.
MATTHEW ARNOLD, *Stanzas in Memory of the Author of Obermann*

I claim not to have controlled events, but confess plainly that events have controlled me.
ABRAHAM LINCOLN, *Speech*, 1864

We had needs invent heaven if it had not been revealed to us.
ROBERT LOUIS STEVENSON, *St. Ives*

The world embarrasses me, and I cannot think
That this watch exists and has no Watchmaker.
VOLTAIRE, *Epigram*

For in him we live, and move, and have our being; as certain
also of your own poets have said, For we are also his offspring.
New Testament: Acts; XVII, 28

(The world) may not look so good, but it is the best God can
do at the time, with conditions as they exist.
JOYCE CARY

We know that all things work together for good to them that
love God.
New Testament: Romans, VIII, 28

God doth not need
Either man's work or his own gifts; who best
Bear his mild yoke, they serve him best; his state
Is kingly. Thousands at his bidding speed
And post o'er land and ocean without rest:
They also serve who only stand and wait.
MILTON, *On His Blindness*

God moves in a mysterious way
His wonders to perform;
He plants his footsteps in the sea,
And rides upon the storm.
WILLIAM COWPER, *Light Shining Out of Darkness*

I believe in God the Father Almighty because wherever I have
looked, through all that I see around me, I see the trace of an
intelligent mind, and because in natural laws, and especially
in the laws which govern the social relations of men, I see, not
merely the proofs of intelligence, but the proofs of beneficence.
HENRY GEORGE

The greatest good of the mind is the knowledge of God.
SPINOZA

OUR COUNTRY

America the Beautiful

The United States themselves are essentially the greatest poem.

WALT WHITMAN, *Leaves of Grass*

O Beautiful! my Country; ours once more!
Smoothing thy gold of war-dishevelled hair
O'er such sweet brows as never others wore.
  And letting thy set lips,
    Freed from wrath's pale eclipse,
The rosy edges of thy smile lay bare,
What words divine of lover or of poet
Could tell our love and make thee know it,
Among the nations bright beyond compare?

JAMES RUSSELL LOWELL, *Commemoration Ode*

America! America!
  God shed His grace on thee
And crown thy good with brotherhood
  From sea to shining sea!

KATHARINE LEE BATES, *America the Beautiful*

Driven from every other corner of the earth, freedom of thought and the right of private judgment in matters of conscience direct their course to this happy country as their last asylum.

SAMUEL ADAMS, *Speech*, 1776

America is God's Crucible, the great Melting-Pot where all the races of Europe are melting and re-forming! God is making the American.

ISRAEL ZANGWILL, *The Melting-Pot*

Bring me men to match my mountains;
  Bring me men to match my plains,—
Men with empires in their purpose,
  And new eras in their brains.

SAM WALTER FOSS, *The Coming American*

A song for our banner! The watchword recall
    Which gave the Republic her station:
"United we stand, divided we fall!"
    It made and preserves us a nation!
The union of lakes, the union of lands,
    The union of States none can sever,
The union of hearts, the union of hands,
    And the flag of our union forever!

GEORGE P. MORRIS, *The Flag of Our Union*

Field and hill and lift and gulch and hollow, mountain and
plain and river, a wilderness with fallen trees across it, a thicket
of bedded brown and twisted undergrowth, a plain, a desert,
and a plantation, a mighty landscape with no fenced niceness,
an immensity of fold and convolution that can never be remembered, that can never be forgotten, that has never been
described—weary with harvest, potent with every fruit and
ore, the immeasurable richness embrowned with autumn, rank,
crude, unharnessed, careless of scars or beauty, everlasting and
magnificent, a cry, a space, an ecstasy!—American earth in
old October.

THOMAS WOLFE, *Of Time and the River*

Lo! body and soul!—this land!
Mighty Manhattan, with spires, and
The sparkling and hurrying tides, and the ships;
The varied and ample land—the South
And the North in the light—Ohio's shores, and flashing
    Missouri,
And ever the far-spreading prairies, covered with grass
    and corn.

WALT WHITMAN

It is a noble land that God has given us: a land that can feed
and clothe the world; a land whose coastlines would enclose
half the countries of Europe; a land set like a sentinel between
the two imperial oceans of the globe, a greater England with a
nobler destiny.

A. J. BEVERIDGE

On Being an American

I feel that you are justified in looking into the future with true assurance, because you have a mode of living in which we find the joy of life and the joy of work harmoniously combined. Added to this is the spirit of ambition which pervades your very being, and seems to make the day's work like a happy child at play.

ALBERT EINSTEIN, 1931

America means opportunity, freedom, power.

RALPH WALDO EMERSON

The eagle's song:
To be staunch, and valiant, and free, and strong.

RICHARD MANSFIELD, *The Eagle's Song*

I believe in the United States of America as a government of the people, by the people, for the people; whose just powers are derived from the consent of the governed; a democracy in a republic; a sovereign nation of many sovereign states; a perfect union, one and inseparable; established upon those principles of freedom, equality, justice and humanity for which American patriots sacrificed their lives and fortunes. I therefore believe it is my duty to my country to love it, to support its constitution, to obey its laws, to respect its flag, and to defend it against all enemies.

WILLIAM TYLER PAGE, *The American's Creed*

When honored and decrepit age shall lean against the base of this monument, and troops of ingenuous youth shall be gathered round it, and when the one shall speak to the other of its objects, the purposes of its construction, and the great and glorious events with which it is connected, there shall rise from every youthful breast the ejaculation, "Thank God, I— I also—am an American!"

DANIEL WEBSTER, *from an address* at the completion of the Bunker Hill Monument

America lives in the heart of every man everywhere who wishes to find a region where he will be free to work out his destiny as he chooses.

WOODROW WILSON

The first requisite of a good citizen in this republic of ours is
that he shall be able and willing to pull his weight.
                                        THEODORE ROOSEVELT

Most Americans are born drunk. They have a sort of permanent intoxication from within, a sort of invisible champagne.
Americans do not need to drink to inspire them to do anything.
                                        G. K. CHESTERTON

I am not a Virginian, but an American.
                                        PATRICK HENRY

The cement of this Union is the heart blood of every American.
                                        THOMAS JEFFERSON, *Writings*

American liberty is a religion. It is a thing of the spirit. It is
an aspiration on the part of people for not alone a free life
but a better life.
                                        WENDELL L. WILLKIE

Destiny has laid upon our country the responsibility of the
free world's leadership.
                                        DWIGHT D. EISENHOWER, *Inaugural Address*

Patriotism

O, Columbia, the gem of the ocean,
    The home of the brave and the free,
The shrine of each patriot's devotion,
    A world offers homage to thee.
                        DAVID T. SHAW AND THOMAS A. BECKET,
                        Columbia, the Gem of the Ocean

Patriotism has its roots deep in the instincts and the affections.
Love of country is the expansion of filial love.
                        D. D. FIELD, *Speeches: A Memorial Address*

He loves his country best who strives to make it best.
        ROBERT G. INGERSOLL, *Decoration Day Oration*, 1882

Let our object be, our country, our whole country, and nothing but our country.

> DANIEL WEBSTER, *from his address*, at the laying
> of the cornerstone of the Bunker Hill Monument

Any relation to the land, the habit of tilling it, or mining it, or even hunting on it, generates the feeling of patriotism.

> RALPH WALDO EMERSON, *The Young American*

Patriotism is easy to understand in America. It means looking out for yourself by looking out for your country.

> CALVIN COOLIDGE

The name of American, which belongs to you in your national capacity, must always exalt the just pride of patriotism more than appellatives derived from local discriminations.

> GEORGE WASHINGTON, *Farewell Address*

Liberty comes alone and lives alone where the hard-won rights of men are held inalienable, where governments themselves may not infringe, where governments are indeed but the mechanisms to protect and sustain these principles. It was this concept for which America's sons have died on a hundred battlefields.

> HERBERT HOOVER

If we win men's hearts throughout the world, it will not be because we are a big country but because we are a great country. Bigness is imposing. But greatness is enduring.

> ADLAI E. STEVENSON, *Address,* February, 1953

Independence Day

While Gen'l Howe with a Large Armament is advancing towards N. York, our Congress resolved to Declare the United Colonies Free and Independent States. A Declaration for this Purpose, I expect, will this day pass Congress. It is gone so far that we must now be a free independent State, or a Conquered Country.

> ABRAHAM CLARKE, a member of the Continental
> Congress from a letter to Elias Dayton July 4, 1776

The second day of July, 1776, will be the most memorable epoch in the history of America. I am apt to believe that it will be celebrated by succeeding generations as the great anniversary festival. It ought to be commemorated as the day of deliverance, by solemn acts of devotion to God Almighty. It ought to be solemnized with pomp and parade, with shows, games, sports, guns, bells, bonfires, and illuminations, from one end of this continent to the other, from this time forward forevermore.

JOHN ADAMS, *Letter to Mrs. Adams,* July 3, 1776

By the rude bridge that arched the flood,
     Their flag to April's breeze unfurled,
Here once the embattled farmers stood,
     And fired the shot heard round the world.
RALPH WALDO EMERSON, *Concord Hymn*

We hold these truths to be self-evident, that all men are created equal, that they are endowed by their Creator with certain unalienable Rights, that among these are Life, Liberty and the pursuit of Happiness. That to secure these rights, Governments are instituted among Men, deriving their just powers from the consent of the governed. That whenever any Form of Government becomes destructive of these ends, it is the Right of the People to alter or to abolish it, and to institute new Government, laying its foundation on such principles and organizing its powers in such form, as to them shall seem most likely to effect their Safety and Happiness. . . . We, therefore, the Representatives of the United States of America, do solemnly publish and declare, That these United Colonies are, and of Right ought to be free and independent States. And for the support of this Declaration, with a firm reliance on the protection of Divine Providence, We mutually pledge to each other our Lives, our Fortunes, and our sacred Honor.

From the *Declaration of Independence,* adopted by the Continental Congress July 4, 1776

Jefferson's Declaration of Independence is a practical document for the use of practical men.

WOODROW WILSON

To-day her thanks shall fly on every wind,
Unstinted, unrebuked, from shore to shore,
One love, one hope, and not a doubt behind!
Cannon to cannon shall repeat her praise,
Banner to banner flap it forth in flame;
Her children shall rise up to bless her name,
And wish her harmless length of days,
The mighty mother of a mighty brood,
Blessed in all tongues and dear to every blood,
The beautiful, the strong, and, best of all, the good.

JAMES RUSSELL LOWELL, *Ode for the Fourth of July*

It is my living sentiment, and by the blessing of God it shall be my dying sentiment,—independence now and independence forever.

DANIEL WEBSTER, *Eulogy on Adams and Jefferson*

Let independence be our boast,
Ever mindful what it cost;
Ever grateful for the prize,
Let its altar reach the skies!

JOSEPH HOPKINSON, *Hail, Columbia!*

The American Flag

I pledge allegiance to the flag of the United States and to the Republic for which it stands, one Nation, indivisible, with Liberty and Justice for all.

JAMES B. UPHAM and FRANCIS M. BELLAMY,
Pledge to the Flag

See the power of national emblems. Some stars, lilies, leopards, a crescent, a lion, an eagle, or other figure which came into credit God knows how, on an old rag of bunting, blowing in the wind on a fort at the ends of the earth, shall make the blood tingle under the rudest or the most conventional exterior.

RALPH WALDO EMERSON, *Essays*

Hats off!
Along the street there comes
A blare of bugles, a ruffle of drums,
A flash of color beneath the sky:
Hats off!
The flag is passing by.

H. H. BENNETT, *The Flag Goes By*

I have seen the glories of art and architecture, and mountain and river; I have seen the sunset on the Jungfrau, and the full moon rise over Mont Blanc; but the fairest vision on which these eyes ever looked was the flag of my country in a foreign land. Beautiful as a flower to those who love it, terrible as a meteor to those who hate it, it is the symbol of the power and glory, and the honor, of fifty millions of Americans.

GEORGE FRISBIE HOAR, *Speech*, 1878

When Freedom from her mountain height
Unfurled her standard to the air,
She tore the azure robe of night,
And set the stars of glory there.
She mingled with its gorgeous dyes
The milky baldric of the skies,
And striped its pure celestial white
With streakings of the morning light.
Then from his mansion in the sun
She called her eagle bearer down,
And gave into his mighty hand
The symbol of her chosen land.

JOSEPH RODMAN DRAKE, *The American Flag*

When I think of the flag, I see alternate strips of parchment upon which are written the rights of liberty and justice, and stripes of blood to vindicate those rights, and then, in the corner, a prediction of the blue serene into which every nation may swim which stands for these great things.

WOODROW WILSON, *Address*, New York, 1915

I am not the flag; not at all. I am but its shadow. I am whatever you make me, nothing more. I am your belief in yourself, your dream of what a People may become. I am the day's work of the weakest man, and the largest dream of the most daring. I am no more than you believe me to be and I am all that you believe I can be. I am whatever you make me, nothing more.

FRANKLIN K. LANE, *Makers of the Flag*

Yes, we'll rally round the flag, boys, we'll rally once again,
    Shouting the battle-cry of Freedom,
We will rally from the hill-side, we'll gather from the plain,
    Shouting the battle-cry of Freedom.

GEORGE F. ROOT, *The Battle-Cry of Freedom*

Oh! thus be it ever, when freemen shall stand
    Between their loved homes and the war's desolation!
Blest with victory and peace, may the heaven-rescued land
    Praise the Power that hath made and preserved us a
        nation.
Then conquer we must, for our cause it is just,
And this be our motto: "In God is our trust."
    And the star-spangled banner in triumph shall wave
    O'er the land of the free and the home of the brave.

FRANCIS SCOTT KEY, *The Star-Spangled Banner*

The Democratic Idea

Democracy arose from men's thinking that if they are equal in any respect, they are equal absolutely.

ARISTOTLE, *Politics*

Democracy is based upon the conviction that there are extraordinary possibilities in ordinary people.

HARRY EMERSON FOSDICK, *Democracy*

Whatever America hopes to bring to pass in the world must first come to pass in the heart of America.

DWIGHT D. EISENHOWER, *Inaugural Address*

The government of the Union, then, is emphatically and truly a government of the people. In form and in substance it emanates from them. Its powers are granted by them, and are to be exercised directly on them and for their benefit.

JOHN MARSHALL, *Case of McCulloch vs. Maryland*, 1819

For there is the democratic idea: that all men are endowed by their creator with certain natural rights; that they are equal as men; and therefore government is to be of all the people, by all the people, and for all the people.

THEODORE PARKER, *Address*, Boston, 1854

It is for us, the living, rather, to be dedicated here to the unfinished work which they who fought here have thus far so nobly advanced. It is rather for us to be here dedicated to the great task remaining before us—that from these honored dead we take increased devotion to that cause for which they gave the last full measure of devotion; that we here highly resolve that these dead shall not have died in vain; that this nation, under God, shall have a new birth of freedom; and that government of the people, by the people, and for the people, shall not perish from the earth.

ABRAHAM LINCOLN, *Gettysburg Address*

President Lincoln defined democracy to be "the government of the people, by the people, for the people." This is a sufficiently compact statement of it as a political arrangement. Theodore Parker said that "Democracy meant not 'I'm as good as you are,' but 'You're as good as I am.'" And this is the ethical conception of it, necessary as a complement of the other.

JAMES RUSSELL LOWELL, *Essays: Democracy*

A representative democracy, where the right of election is well secured and regulated, and the exercise of the legislature, executive, and judiciary authorities is vested in select persons, chosen really and not nominally by the people, will, in my opinion, be most likely to be happy, regular, and durable.

ALEXANDER HAMILTON, *Works*, Vol. IX

I know no safe depository of the ultimate powers of society but the people themselves; and if we think them not enlightened enough to exercise their control with a wholesome discretion, the remedy is not to take it from them, but to inform their discretion by education.

THOMAS JEFFERSON, *Letter to W. C. Jarvis*, Sept. 28, 1820

To do justice to all and to submit to wrong from none has been during my administration its growing maxim, and so happy have been its results that we are not only at peace with all the world, but have few causes of controversy, and those of minor importance, remaining unadjusted.

ANDREW JACKSON, *Second Inaugural Address*

I speak the pass-word primeval, I give the sign of democracy,
By God! I will accept nothing which all cannot have their
counterpart of on the same terms.

WALT WHITMAN, *Song of Myself*

The beauty of a Democracy is that you never can tell when a youngster is born what he is going to do with you, and that, no matter how humbly he is born he has got a chance to master the minds and lead the imaginations of the whole country.

WOODROW WILSON, *Address*, Columbus, Ohio, 1915

He who takes the oath today to preserve, protect and defend the Constitution of the United States only assumes the solemn obligation which every patriotic citizen—on the farm, in the workshop, in the busy marts of trade, and everywhere—should share with him. The Constitution which prescribes his oath, my countrymen, is yours; the government you have chosen him to administer for a time is yours; the suffrage which executes the will of free men is yours; the laws and the entire scheme of our civil rule, from the town meeting to the state capitols and the national capitol, is yours.

GROVER CLEVELAND, *Inaugural Address*, 1885

It would be folly to argue that the people cannot make political mistakes. They can and do make grave mistakes. They know it, they pay the penalty, but compared with the mistakes which have been made by every kind of autocracy they are unimportant.

CALVIN COOLIDGE, *Speech*, 1923

The Founding Fathers

Washington is the mightiest name of earth—long since mightiest in the cause of civil liberty, still mightiest in moral reformation. On that name no eulogy is expected. It cannot be.

To add brightness to the sun or glory to the name of Washington is alike impossible. Let none attempt it. In solemn awe pronounce the name, and in its naked deathless splendor leave it shining on.

ABRAHAM LINCOLN, from an address at
Springfield, Ill., Feb. 22, 1842

A citizen, first in war, first in peace, and first in the hearts of his countrymen.

HENRY (Light-Horse Harry) LEE, from resolutions adopted by the Congress on the death of Washington, 1799

Washington, the brave, the wise, the good,
Supreme in war, in council, and in peace,
Valiant without ambition, discreet without fear,
Confident without presumption.
In disaster, calm; in success, moderate; in all, himself.
The hero, the patriot, the Christian.
The father of nations, the friend of mankind,
Who, when he had won all, renounced all,
And sought in the bosom of his family and of nature, retirement,
And in the hope of religion, immortality.

UNKNOWN, *Inscription on Washington's Tomb*

That name descending with all time, spreading over the whole earth, and uttered in all the languages belonging to all tribes and races of men, will forever be pronounced with affectionate gratitude by everyone in whose breast there shall arise an aspiration for human rights and liberty.

DANIEL WEBSTER, *Speech*, Centennial Anniversary
of Washington, Feb. 22, 1832

Soldier and statesman, rarest unison;
High-poised example of great duties done
Simply as breathing, a world's honors worn
As life's indifferent gifts to all men born;
Not honored then or now because he wooed
The popular voice, but that he still withstood;
Broad-minded, higher-souled, there is but one
Who was all this and ours, and all men's—Washington.

JAMES RUSSELL LOWELL, *Under the Old Elm*

O Washington!—thrice glorious name,
   What due rewards can man decree—
Empires are far below thy aims,
   And sceptres have no charms for thee.
PHILIP FRENEAU, *Occasioned by General Washington's
Arrival at Philadelphia*

The character, the counsels, and example of our Washington will guide us through the doubts and difficulties that beset us; they will guide our children and our children's children in the paths of prosperity and peace, while America shall hold her place in the family of nations.
EDWARD EVERETT, *Speech: Washington Abroad and at Home*

Were an energetic and judicious system to be proposed with your signature it would be a circumstance highly honorable to your fame and doubly entitle you to the glorious republican epithet, The Father of your Country.
HENRY KNOX, *Letter to Washington*, March 19, 1787

On the whole his character was, in its mass, perfect, in nothing bad, in few points indifferent; and it may truly be said that never did nature and fortune combine more perfectly to make a man great.
THOMAS JEFFERSON, *Writings* (on Washington)

It is hardly necessary to state that Franklin did not originate all the "Sayings of Poor Richard." He himself tells us that they were "the wisdom of many ages and nations." Yet with but few exceptions these maxims and aphorisms had been filtered through Franklin's brain, and were tinged with that mother wit which so strongly and individually marks so much that he said and wrote.
PAUL LEICESTER FORD, *The Sayings
of Poor Richard: Introduction*

But matchless Franklin! What a few
Can hope to rival such as you.
Who seized from kings their sceptred pride
And turned the lightning's darts aside.
PHILIP FRENEAU, *On the Death of Benjamin Franklin*

He snatched the thunderbolt from heaven, the sceptre from tyrants.
A. R. J. TURGOT

I succeed him; no one could replace him.

THOMAS JEFFERSON, to the Comte de Vergennes, when the latter remarked, "You replace Mr. Franklin," as envoy to France.

The immortality of Thomas Jefferson does not lie in any one of his achievements, but in his attitude toward mankind.

WOODROW WILSON, *Speech*, Washington, 1916

He had a steadfast and abiding faith in justice, righteousness and liberty as the prevailing and abiding forces in the conduct of States, and that justice and righteousness were sure to prevail where any people bear rule in perfect liberty.

GEORGE F. HOAR, *Thomas Jefferson*

A gentleman of thirty-two who could calculate an eclipse, survey an estate, tie an artery, plan an edifice, try a cause, break a horse, dance a minuet and play the violin.

JAMES PARTON, *Life of Jefferson*

Here was buried Thomas Jefferson, author of the Declaration of American Independence, of the statute of Virginia for religious freedom, and father of the University of Virginia.

THOMAS JEFFERSON, *Epitaph*, written for himself

I have the consolation to reflect that during the period of my administration not a drop of the blood of a single fellow citizen was shed by the sword of war or of the law.

THOMAS JEFFERSON, *Writings*

Abraham Lincoln

His heart was as great as the world, but there was no room in it to hold the memory of a wrong.

RALPH WALDO EMERSON, *Letters and Social Aims: Greatness*

> Oh, slow to smite and swift to spare,
>   Gentle and merciful and just!
> Who, in the fear of God, didst bear
>   The sword of power, a nation's trust!

WILLIAM CULLEN BRYANT, *Abraham Lincoln*

The color of the ground was in him, the red earth,
The smack and tang of elemental things:
The rectitude and patience of the cliff,
The goodwill of the rain that loves all leaves,
The friendly welcome of the wayside well,
The courage of the bird that dares the sea,
The gladness of the wind that shakes the corn,
The pity of the snow that hides all scars,
The tolerance and equity of light.

> EDWIN MARKHAM, *Lincoln, The Man of the People*

That nation has not lived in vain which has given the world Washington and Lincoln, the best great men and the greatest good men whom history can show.

> HENRY CABOT LODGE, *Lincoln.* Address before
> Massachusetts Legislature, Feb. 12, 1909

Unheralded, God's captain came
As one that answers to his name;
Nor dreamed how high his charge,
His privilege how large.

> JOHN VANCE CHENEY, *Lincoln*

May one who fought in honor for the
    South
Uncovered stand and sing by Lincoln's
    grave?
. . . A soft Kentucky strain was in his voice,
And the Ohio's deeper boom was there,
With some wild accents of old Wabash
    days,
    And winds of Illinois;
And when he spoke he took us unaware,
With his high courage and unselfish
    ways.

> MAURICE THOMPSON, *At Lincoln's Grave*

Blackguard and buffoon as he is, he has pursued his end with an energy as untiring as an Indian, and a singleness of purpose that might almost be called patriotic.

> ANON In Charleston Mercury, Jan. 10, 1865

Strange mingling of mirth and tears, of the tragic and grotesque, of cap and crown, of Socrates and Rabelais, of Aesop and Marcus Aurelius—Lincoln, the gentlest memory of the world.

ROBERT G. INGERSOLL, Lincoln

> For he, to whom we had applied
> Our shopman's test of age and worth,
> Was elemental when he died,
> As he was ancient at his birth:
> The saddest among kings of earth,
> Bowed with a galling crown, this man
> Met rancor with a cryptic mirth,
> Laconic—and Olympian.
> EDWIN ARLINGTON ROBINSON, The Master

Lincoln was a very normal man with very normal gifts, but all upon a great scale, all knit together in loose and natural form, like the great frame in which he moved and dwelt.

WOODROW WILSON, Address, Chicago, Feb. 12, 1909

O Captain! my Captain! our fearful trip is done,
The ship has weather'd every rack, the prize we sought is won,
The port is near, the bells I hear, the people all exulting,
While follow eyes the steady keel, the vessel grim and daring;
But O heart! heart! heart!
O the bleeding drops of red,
Where on the deck my Captain lies,
Fallen cold and dead.
WALT WHITMAN, O Captain! My Captain!

Now he belongs to the ages.
EDWIN M. STANTON, upon the death of Lincoln, April 15, 1865

Famous Sayings from Our History

E Pluribus Unum. (One from many.)
(Motto for seal of the United States, proposed by BENJAMIN FRANKLIN, JOHN ADAMS, and THOMAS JEFFERSON, and adopted June 20, 1782)

Liberty and Union, now and forever, one and inseparable!
DANIEL WEBSTER, (1830)

Men, you are all marksmen—don't one of you fire until you
see the white of their eyes.
ISRAEL PUTNAM, (at Battle of Bunker Hill, 1775)

I only regret that I have but one life to lose for my country.
NATHAN HALE, (spoken upon the gallows just before
being hanged as a spy by the British, New York, 1776)

Don't give up the ship!
COMMODORE OLIVER HAZARD PERRY,
(during the battle of Lake Erie, 1813)

Don't tread on me.
(On the first flag of the Revolution, showing
a pine tree and a rattlesnake, used on
John Paul Jones's ship, 1776)

These are the times that try men's souls.
THOMAS PAINE, *The Crisis*

I have not yet begun to fight.
JOHN PAUL JONES, (when his ship, the
Bonhomme Richard, was sinking while fighting
the British *Serapis*, 1779)

Millions for defense but not one cent for tribute.
ROBERT GOODLOE HARPER,
(upon his return from France in 1798)

We have met the enemy and they are ours.
OLIVER HAZARD PERRY,
(announcing victory, battle of Lake Erie, 1813)

I propose to fight it out on this line if it takes all summer.
ULYSSES S. GRANT, (1864)

Damn the torpedoes! Go ahead!
DAVID GLASGOW FARRAGUT, (Mobile Bay, 1864)

Remember the Maine!
(referring to destruction of the battleship Maine, 1898)

Lafayette, we are here.
COLONEL C. E. STANTON,
(at the grave of Lafayette in Paris, 1917, upon arrival of
American Expeditionary Forces in France)

The only thing we have to fear is fear itself.
FRANKLIN DELANO ROOSEVELT,
(from First Inaugural Address, 1933)

Explorers and Pioneers

Columbus found a world, and had no chart,
Save one that faith deciphered in the skies;
To trust the soul's invincible surmise
Was all his science and his only art.
GEORGE SANTAYANA, *O World*

He gained a world; he gave that world
Its grandest lesson: "On! sail on!"
JOAQUIN MILLER, *Columbus*

God, the Guider of all good actions, forcing them by an
extreme storm to hull all night, did drive them by his Providence to their desired port, beyond all their expectations;
for never had any of them seen that coast.
CAPTAIN JOHN SMITH, the Founding of Jamestown, 1607

(After the Battle of Lexington.) Samuel Adams, with the
voice of a prophet, exclaimed: "Oh, what a glorious morning
is this!" for he saw his country's independence hastening on,
and, like Columbus in the tempest, knew that the storm bore
him more swiftly toward the undiscovered world.
GEORGE BANCROFT, *History of the United States*
(published, 1840)

Shall I tell you who he is, this key figure in the arch of our
enterprise? That slender, dauntless, plodding, modest figure is
the American pioneer.
FRANKLIN K. LANE, *The American Pioneer*

Conquering, holding, daring, venturing as we go the
    unknown ways,
Pioneers! O pioneers!
        WALT WHITMAN, *Pioneers! O Pioneers*

    His echoing axe the settler swung
        Amid the sea-like solitude,
    And, rushing, thundering, down were flung
        The Titans of the wood.
        ALFRED B. STREET, *The Settler*

    Out where the handclasp's a little stronger,
    Out where the smile dwells a little longer,
        That's where the West begins.
        ARTHUR CHAPMAN, *Out Where the West Begins*

Go West, young man, and grow up with the country.
        HORACE GREELEY

HOME AND FAMILY

The Dearest Place

Where we love is home,
Home that our feet may leave, but not our hearts.
OLIVER WENDELL HOLMES, *Homesick in Heaven*

But what on earth is half so dear—
So longed for—as the hearth of home?
EMILY BRONTÉ, *A Little While*

Whom God loves, his house is sweet to him.
CERVANTES, *Don Quixote*

Of a' roads to happiness ever were tried,
There's nane half so sure as ane's ain fireside.
ELIZABETH HAMILTON, *My Ain Fireside*

And I am praying God on high,
And I am praying Him night and day,
For a little house—a house of my own—
Out of the wind's and the rain's way.
PADRAIC COLUM, *An Old Woman of the Roads*

For home, though homely 'twere, yet it is sweet.
ARIOSTO, *Orlando Furioso*

Is not a small house best? Put a woman into a small house,
and after five years she comes out large and healthy.
RALPH WALDO EMERSON, *Journals*

'Mid pleasures and palaces though we may roam,
Be it ever so humble, there's no place like home.
JOHN HOWARD PAYNE, *Home Sweet Home*

A little house well fill'd, a little land well till'd, and a little
wife well will'd, are great riches.
JOHN RAY, *English Proverbs*

God oft hath a great share in a little house.
GEORGE HERBERT, *Jacula Prudentum*

75

They shall sit every man under his vine and under his fig tree.
Old Testament: Micah, IV, 4

Nor hell nor heaven shall that soul surprise,
    Who loves the rain,
    And loves his home,
And looks on life with quiet eyes.
FRANCES SHAW, *Who Loves the Rain*

'Tis sweet to hear the watch-dog's honest bark
    Bay deep-mouth'd welcome as we draw near home;
'Tis sweet to know there is an eye will mark
    Our coming, and look brighter when we come.
BYRON, *Don Juan*

Any old place I can hang my hat is home, sweet home to me.
WILLIAM JEROME and JEAN SCHWARTZ
(from a popular song of 1901)

To be happy at home is the ultimate result of all ambition,
the end to which every enterprise and labor tends, and of
which every desire prompts the prosecution.
SAMUEL JOHNSON, *The Rambler*

The Art of Hospitality

Hospitality consists in a little fire, a little food, and an im-
mense quiet.

EMERSON, *Journal*

Be not forgetful to entertain strangers: for thereby some have
entertained angels unawares.
New Testament: Hebrews, XIII, 2

In good company you need not ask who is the master of the
feast. The man who sits in the lowest place, and who is always
industrious in helping every one, is certainly the man.
DAVID HUME, *Essays: Rise and Progress of Arts*

Stay is a charming word in a friend's vocabulary.
AMOS BRONSON ALCOTT, *Concord Days: June*

Come in the evening, or come in the morning,
Come when you're looked for, or come without warning,
Kisses and welcome you'll find here before you,
And the oftener you come here the more I'll adore you.
                    THOMAS O. DAVIS, *The Welcome*

Hail Guest! We ask not what thou art:
If Friend, we greet thee, hand and heart;
If Stranger, such no longer be;
If Foe, our love shall conquer thee. *
                    ARTHUR GUITERMAN, *Old Welsh Door Verse*

You must come home with me and be my guest;
You will give joy to me, and I will do
All that is in my power to honour you.
                    PERCY BYSSHE SHELLEY, *Hymn to Mercury*

There is an emanation from the heart in genuine hospitality
which cannot be described, but is immediately felt and puts
the stranger at once at his ease.

                    WASHINGTON IRVING

A Garden Fair

Who loves a garden still his Eden keeps,
Perennial pleasure plants, and wholesome harvests reaps.
                    AMOS BRONSON ALCOTT, *Tablets: The Garden*

A garden is a lovesome thing, God wot!
Rose plot, Fringed pool, Ferned grot—
      The veriest school
      Of peace; and yet the fool
Contends that God is not.
Not God! in gardens! when the eve is cool?
      Nay, but I have a sign:
      'Tis very sure God walks in mine.
                    THOMAS EDWARD BROWN, *My Garden*

---

* From *Death and General Putnam and 101 Other Poems* by
Arthur Guiterman. Published and copyright, 1935, E. P. Dutton &
Co., Inc., N. Y.

God Almighty first planted a garden. And, indeed, it is the purest of human pleasures.

FRANCIS BACON, *Essays: Of Gardens*

O the green things growing, the green things growing,
The faint sweet smell of the green things growing!
I should like to live, whether I smile or grieve,
Just to watch the happy life of my green things growing.

DINAH MULOCK CRAIK, *Green Things Growing*

I never had any other desire so strong and so like to covetousness, as that one which I have had always, that I might be master at last of a small house and large garden.

ABRAHAM COWLEY, *The Garden*

Fathers and Sons

He that honoureth his father shall have a long life.

Apocrypha: Ecclesiasticus, III, 6

One father is more than a hundred schoolmasters.

GEORGE HERBERT, *Jacula Prudentum*

It's a wise child that knows its own father.

HOMER, *Odyssey*

The night my father got me
His mind was not on me;
He did not plague his fancy
To muse if I should be
The son you see.

A. E. HOUSMAN, *Last Poems*

Like father, like son: every good tree maketh good fruits.

WILLIAM LANGLAND, *Piers Plowman*

A wise son maketh a glad father.

Old Testament: Proverbs, X, 1

It is not flesh and blood but the heart which makes us fathers and sons.

SCHILLER, *Die Räuber*

To you your father should be as a god;
One that composed your beauties, yea, and one
To whom you are but as a form in wax
By him imprinted and within his power
To leave the figure or disfigure it.
> SHAKESPEARE, *A Midsummer-Night's Dream*

O dearest, dearest boy! my heart
For better lore would seldom yearn,
Could I but teach the hundredth part
Of what from thee I learn.
> WILLIAM WORDSWORTH, *Anecdote for Fathers*

What greater ornament to a son than a father's glory, or to a father than a son's honorable conduct?
> SOPHOCLES, *Antigone*

The survivorship of a worthy man in his son is a pleasure scarce inferior to the hopes of the continuance of his own life.
> RICHARD STEELE, *The Spectator*

Husband and Wife

A good husband makes a good wife.
> ROBERT BURTON, *Anatomy of Melancholy*

With thee goes
Thy husband, him to follow thou art bound;
Where he abides, think there thy native soil.
> JOHN MILTON, *Paradise Lost*

Thy husband is thy lord, thy life, thy keeper,
Thy head, thy sovereign; one that cares for thee,
And for thy maintenance commits his body
To painful labour both by sea and land,
To watch the night in storms, the day in cold,
Whilst thou liest warm at home, secure and safe;
And craves no other tribute at thy hands
But love, fair looks and true obedience.
> SHAKESPEARE, *Taming of the Shrew*

Every man who is high up loves to think he has done it all himself; and the wife smiles, and lets it go at that. It's only our joke. Every woman knows that.

JAMES M. BARRIE, *What Every Woman Knows*

The wife is the key of the house.

THOMAS FULLER, *Gnomologia*

Maids must be wives and mothers to fulfil
The entire and holiest end of woman's being.

FRANCES ANNE KEMBLE, *Woman's Heart*

An ideal wife is any woman who has an ideal husband.

BOOTH TARKINGTON, *Looking Forward*

A man is in general better pleased when he has a good dinner upon his table, than when his wife talks Greek.

SAMUEL JOHNSON, *Miscellanies*

No happiness is like unto it, no love so great as that of man and wife, no such comfort as a sweet wife.

ROBERT BURTON, *Anatomy of Melancholy*

What is there in the vale of life
Half so delightful as a wife,
When friendship, love, and peace combine
To stamp the marriage bond divine?

WILLIAM COWPER, *Love Abused*

Every wise man loves the wife he has chosen.

HOMER, *Iliad*

When a man dwells in love, then the breasts of his wife are pleasant as the droppings upon the hill of Hermon, her eyes are fair as the light of Heaven, she is a fountain sealed, and he can quench his thirst, and ease his cares, and lay his sorrow down upon her lap, and can retire home as to his sanctuary and refectory, and his garden of sweetness and chaste refreshment.

JEREMY TAYLOR, *The Mysteriousness of Marriage*

We poor common people must take wives whom we love and who love us.

MOZART, Letter to his father

Her children arise up and call her blessed; her husband also, and he praiseth her.

Old Testament: Proverbs xxxi, 28

He knew whose gentle hand was at the latch,
Before the door had given her to his eyes.

KEATS, *Isabella*

She who ne'er answers till a husband cools,
Or, if she rules him, never shows she rules.
Charms by accepting, by submitting sways,
Yet has her humour most when she obeys.

ALEXANDER POPE, *Moral Essays*

A good wife and health are man's best wealth.

JOHN RAY, *English Proverbs*

Children

Children divine those who love them; it is a gift of nature which we lose as we grow up.

PAUL DE KOCK, *L'Homme aux Trois Culottes*

In praise of little children I will say
God first made man, then found a better way
For woman, but his third way was the best.
Of all created things, the loveliest
And most divine are children.

WILLIAM CANTON, *Laus Infantium*

Of all nature's gifts to the human race, what is sweeter to a man than his children?

CICERO, *Post Reditum ad Quirites*

Evening, thou that bringest all that bright morning scattered;
thou bringest the sheep, the goat, the child back to its mother.

SAPPHO

One laugh of a child will make the holiest day more sacred still.

ROBERT G. INGERSOLL, *The Liberty of Man, Woman and Child*

> Blessings on thee, little man
> Barefoot boy with cheek of tan.
> JOHN GREENLEAF WHITTIER, *Barefoot Boy*

Lo, children are a heritage of the Lord: and the fruit of the womb is his reward. As arrows are in the hand of a mighty man, so are children of the youth. Happy is the man that hath his quiver full of them.

Old Testament: Psalms, CXXVII, 3-5

> If there is anything that will endure
> The eye of God, because it still is pure,
> It is the spirit of a little child,
> Fresh from his hand, and therefore undefiled.
> RICHARD HENRY STODDARD, *The Children's Prayer*

Children think not of what is past, nor what is to come, but enjoy the present time, which few of us do.

LA BRUYÈRE, *Les Caractères*

> A rose with all its sweetest leaves yet folded.

BYRON

Children are God's apostles, day by day sent forth to preach of love and hope and peace.

JAMES RUSSELL LOWELL

Blessed be the hand that prepares a pleasure for a child, for there is no saying when and where it may bloom forth.

DOUGLAS JERROLD

Call not that man wretched, who, whatever else he suffers as to pain inflicted or pleasure denied, has a child for whom he hopes and on whom he dotes.

SAMUEL TAYLOR COLERIDGE

Advice to Parents

Respect the child. Be not too much his parent. Trespass not on his solitude.
RALPH WALDO EMERSON, *Lectures and Biographical Sketches*

Children have more need of models than of critics.
JOSEPH JOUBERT, *Pensées*

What good mothers and fathers instinctively feel like doing for their babies is best after all.
DR. BENJAMIN M. SPOCK, *The Common Sense Book of Baby and Child Care*

Whilst that the child is young, let him be instructed in virtue and literature.
JOHN LYLY, *Euphues: Of the Education of Youth*

Train up a child in the way he should go; and when he is old, he will not depart from it.
Old Testament: Proverbs, XXII, 6

It is better to bind your children to you by respect and gentleness, than by fear.
TERENCE, *Adelphi*

Happy is he that is happy in his children.
THOMAS FULLER, *Gnomologia*

The joys of parents are secret, and so are their griefs and fears.
FRANCIS BACON, *Essays*

What power there is in the smile of a child, in its play, in its crying—in short, in its mere existence. Are you able to resist its demand? Or do you hold out to it, as a mother, your breast, or, as a father, whatever it needs of your belongings?
MAX STIRNER, *The Ego and His Own*

Give a little love to a child, and you get a great deal back.
JOHN RUSKIN, *The Crown of Wild Olive*

If parents carry it lovingly towards their children, mixing their mercies with loving rebukes, and their loving rebukes with fatherly and motherly compassions, they are more likely to save their children than by being churlish and severe towards them.

JOHN BUNYAN, *The Life and Death of Mr. Badman*

Children naturally want to be like their parents, and to do what they do.

WILLIAM COBBETT, *Advice to Young Men*

To season them, and win them early to the love of virtue and true labor, ere any flattering seducement or vain principle seize them wandering, some easy and delightful book of education should be read to them.

JOHN MILTON

Motherhood

All that I am or hope to be, I owe to my angel mother.

ABRAHAM LINCOLN

The bearing and the training of a child
Is woman's wisdom.

ALFRED TENNYSON, *The Princess*

Womanliness means only motherhood;
All love begins and ends there,—roams enough,
But, having run the circle, rests at home.

ROBERT BROWNING, *The Inn Album*

There is none,
In all this cold and hollow world, no fount
Of deep, strong, deathless love, save that within
A mother's heart.

FELICIA HEMANS, *The Siege of Valencia*

The bravest battle that ever was fought;
Shall I tell you where and when?

On the maps of the world you will find it not;
    It was fought by the mothers of men.
                JOAQUIN MILLER, *The Bravest Battle*

The angels—singing unto one another,
Can find amid their burning terms of love,
None so devotional as that of "mother."
                EDGAR ALLAN POE, *To My Mother*

Is not a young mother one of the sweetest sights life shows us?
                THACKERAY, *The Newcomes*

They say that man is mighty,
    He governs land and sea,
He wields a mighty scepter
    O'er lesser powers that be;
But a mightier power and stronger
    Man from his throne has hurled,
For the hand that rocks the cradle
    Is the hand that rules the world.
      WILLIAM ROSS WALLACE, *What Rules the World*

Her children arise up and call her blessed.
              Old Testament: Proverbs, xxxi, 28

Motherhood is the keystone of the arch of matrimonial happiness.

              THOMAS JEFFERSON,
      Letter to Martha Jefferson Randolph, 1791

A mother's prayers, silent and gentle, can never miss the road to the throne of all bounty.

              HENRY WARD BEECHER

I give you mom. I give you the destroying mother . . . I give you the angel—and point to the sword in her hand . . . Our society is too much an institution built to appease the rapacity of loving mothers.

          PHILIP WYLIE, *Generation of Vipers*

The tie which links mother and child is of such pure and immaculate strength as to be never violated, except by those whose feelings are withered by vitiated society. Holy, simple, and beautiful in its construction, it is the emblem of all we can imagine of fidelity and truth.

WASHINGTON IRVING

Mighty is the force of motherhood! It transforms all things by its vital heat; it turns timidity into fierce courage, and dreadless defiance into tremulous submission; it turns thoughtlessness into foresight, and yet stills all anxiety into calm content; it makes selfishness become self-denial, and gives even to hard vanity the glance of admiring love.

GEORGE ELIOT

Sisters and Daughters

For there is no friend like a sister,
In calm or stormy weather,
To cheer one on the tedious way,
To fetch one if one goes astray,
To lift one if one totters down,
To strengthen whilst one stands.

CHRISTINA GEORGINA ROSSETTI, *Goblin Market*

My sister! my sweet sister! if a name
Dearer and purer were, it should be thine.

BYRON, *Epistle to Augusta*

A ministering angel shall my sister be.

SHAKESPEARE, *Hamlet*

Reproof a parent's province is;
A sister's discipline is this:
By studied kindness to effect
A little brother's young respect.

MARY LAMB, *The Broken Doll*

The companion, the friend, and confidant of her mother, and the object of a pleasure something like the love between the angels to her father.

RICHARD STEELE, *The Tatler*

The younger your daughter, the more apt she is to love you.
E. W. HOWE, *Country Town Sayings*

The lucky man has a daughter as his first child.
Spanish Proverb

Nothing is dearer to an old father than a daughter. Sons have spirits of higher pitch, but they are not given to fondness.
EURIPIDES, *The Suppliant Woman*

Thy daughters bright thy walks adorn,
Gay as the gilded summer sky,
Sweet as the dewy, milk-white thorn,
Dear as the raptured thrill of joy.
ROBERT BURNS, *Address to Edinburgh*

A lady with her daughters or her nieces
Shines like a guinea and seven-shilling pieces.
BYRON, *Don Juan*

Filled her with thee, a daughter fair,
So buxom, blithe, and debonair.
MILTON, *L'Allegro*

Trust to me, judicious mother: do not make of your daughter an honest man, as if to give the lie to Nature; make her an honest woman, and be assured that she will be of more worth both to herself and to us.

ROUSSEAU

It is harder to marry a daughter well than to bring her up well.
THOMAS FULLER, *Gnomologia*

O loveliest daughter of a lovely mother.
HORACE, *Carmina*

Childhood's Delights

The hills are dearest which our childish feet
Have climbed the earliest; and the streams most sweet
Are ever those at which our young lips drank.
JOHN GREENLEAF WHITTIER, *The Bridal of Pennacook*

What art can paint or gild any object in after life with the glow which nature gives to the first baubles of childhood? St. Peter's cannot have the magical power over us that the red and gold covers of our first picture-book possessed.

RALPH WALDO EMERSON, *Domestic Life*

One of the greatest pleasures of childhood is found in the mysteries which it hides from the skepticism of the elders, and works up into small mythologies of its own.

OLIVER WENDELL HOLMES

Happy season of childhood! Kind Nature, that art to all a bountiful mother; that visitest the poor man's hut with auroral radiance; and for thy nursling hast provided a soft swathing of love and infinite hope wherein he waxes and slumbers, danced round by sweetest dreams!

THOMAS CARLYLE

Childhood, whose very happiness is love.

LETITIA ELIZABETH LANDON, *Erinna*

The greatest poem ever known
Is one all poets have outgrown:
The poetry, innate, untold,
Of being only four years old.*

CHRISTOPHER MORLEY, *To a Child*

How dear to this heart are the scenes of my childhood,
    When fond recollection recalls them to view;
The orchard, the meadow, the deep-tangled wildwood,
    And every loved spot which my infancy knew.

SAMUEL WOODWORTH, *The Old Oaken Bucket*

There was a time when meadow, grove, and stream,
The earth, and every common sight,
    To me did seem
Apparelled in celestial light.

WILLIAM WORDSWORTH, *Ode on the Intimations of Immortality*

* From *Chimney Smoke* by Christopher Morley. Copyright, 1921, 1949 by Christopher Morley. Published by J. B. Lippincott Co.

Between the dark and the daylight,
    When the night is beginning to lower,
Comes a pause in the day's occupations,
    That is known as the Children's Hour.
            LONGFELLOW, *The Children's Hour*

O Life! how pleasant is thy morning,
Young Fancy's rays the hills adorning!
Cold-pausing Caution's lesson scorning,
    We frisk away,
Like schoolboys at th' expected warning,
    To joy an' play.
            ROBERT BURNS, *Epistle to James Smith*

We were as twinn'd lambs that did frisk i' the sun,
And bleat the one at the other; what we chang'd
Was innocence for innocence; we knew not
The doctrine of ill-doing, nor dream'd
That any did.
            SHAKESPEARE, *The Winter's Tale*

The heart of childhood is all mirth:
    We frolic to and fro
As free and blithe, as if on earth
    Were no such thing as woe.
            JOHN KEBLE, *The Christian Year*

Without, the frost, the blinding snow,
    The storm-wind's moody madness—
Within, the firelight's ruddy glow
    And childhood's nest of gladness.
            LEWIS CARROLL, *Through the Looking-Glass:*
                           Introduction

I devise to children the banks of the brooks and the golden
sands beneath the waters thereof, and the odors of the willows
that dip therein, and the white clouds that float high over the
giant trees. And I leave to them the long days to be merry in,
in a thousand ways, and the night and the moon, and the train
of the Milky Way to wonder at.
            CHARLES LOUNSBURY, *Last will and testament*

SELF-IMPROVEMENT, CHARACTER AND PERSONALITY

Confidence in Yourself

Go to your bosom;
Knock there, and ask your heart what it doth know.
> SHAKESPEARE, *Measure for Measure*

Once read thy own breast right,
And thou hast done with fears!
Man gets no other light,
Search he a thousand years.
> MATTHEW ARNOLD, *Empedocles on Etna*

O wad some Pow'r the giftie gie us
To see oursels as ithers see us!
It wad frae monie a blunder free us.—
An' foolish notion:
What airs in dress an' gait wad lea'e us,
An' ev'n devotion!
> ROBERT BURNS, *To a Louse*

Great God, I ask thee for no meaner pelf
Than that I may not disappoint myself.
> HENRY DAVID THOREAU, *My Prayer*

What you think of yourself is much more important than what others think of you.

> SENECA, *Epistulae ad Lucilium*

If you tell me how you get your feeling of importance, I'll tell you what you are. That determines your character. That is the most significant thing about you.
> DALE CARNEGIE, *How to Win Friends and Influence People*

Men who know themselves are no longer fools; they stand on the threshold of the Door of Wisdom.
> HAVELOCK ELLIS, *Impressions and Comments*

Love yourself and your own affairs without any rival.
> HORACE, *Ars Poetica*

It is necessary to the happiness of man that he be mentally faithful to himself.

THOMAS PAINE, *The Age of Reason*

I have forgotten how to sigh—
Remembered how to sleep.

DOROTHY PARKER

Self-confidence is the first requisite to great undertakings.

SAMUEL JOHNSON

There is no dependence that can be sure but a dependence upon one's self.

JOHN GAY, *Letter to Swift*

Confidence is that feeling by which the mind embarks in great and honorable courses with a sure hope and trust in itself.

CICERO, *De Inventione Rhetorica*

Some men are just as firmly convinced of what they think as others are of what they know.

ARISTOTLE, *Nicomachean Ethics*

The Value of Education

Education is the only interest worthy the deep, controlling anxiety of the thoughtful man.

WENDELL PHILLIPS, *Speeches: Idols*

Studies serve for delight, for ornament, and for ability.

FRANCIS BACON, *Essays*

I call, therefore, a complete and generous education, that which fits a man to perform justly, skillfully and magnanimously all the offices, both public and private, of peace and war.

JOHN MILTON, *On Education*

Education alone can conduct us to that enjoyment which is at once best in quality and infinite in quantity.

HORACE MANN, *Lectures and Reports on Education*

Most Americans do value education as a business asset, but not as the entrance into the joy of intellectual experience or acquaintance with the best that has been said and done in the past. They value it not as an experience, but as a tool.

W. H. P. FAUNCE, *Letter to Abraham Flexner*, Jan. 16, 1928

'Tis education forms the common mind;
Just as the twig is bent the tree's inclined.

ALEXANDER POPE, *Moral Essays*

It is in education more than anywhere else that we have sincerely striven to carry into execution "the Great American Dream": the vision of a longer and fuller life for the ordinary man, a life of widened freedom, of equal opportunity for each to make of himself all that he is capable of becoming.

JOHN DEWEY

Instruction increases inborn worth, and right discipline strengthens the heart.

HORACE, *Odes*

It was in making education not only common to all but in some sense compulsory to all that the destiny of the free republics of America was practically settled.

JAMES RUSSELL LOWELL, *New England Two Centuries Ago*

The only really educated men are self-educated.

JESSE LEE BENNETT, *Culture and A Liberal Education*

Education is leading human souls to what is best, and no crime can destroy, no enemy can alienate, no despotism can enslave. At home a friend, abroad an introduction, in solitude a solace, and in society an ornament. It chastens vice, it guides virtue, it gives at once grace and government to genius. Without it, what is man? A splendid slave, a reasoning savage.

JOSEPH ADDISON, *The Spectator*

Education is the leading human souls to what is best, and making what is best out of them; and these two objects are always attainable together, and by the same means; the training which makes men happiest in themselves also makes them most serviceable to others.

JOHN RUSKIN, *Stones of Venice*

The heart of the problem of a general education is the continuance of the liberal and humane tradition. Neither the mere acquisition of information nor the development of special skills and talents can give the broad basis of understanding which is essential if our civilization is to be preserved.

JAMES BRYANT CONANT, *Introduction to General Education in a Free Society*

Rewards of Honesty and Patience

Divine Providence has granted this gift to man, that those things which are honest are also the most advantageous.

QUINTILIAN, *De Institutione Oratoria*

No legacy is so rich as honesty.

SHAKESPEARE, *All's Well that Ends Well*

An honest man is the noblest work of God.

POPE, *Essay on Man*

I hope I shall always possess firmness and virtue enough to maintain what I consider the most enviable of all titles, the character of an Honest Man.

GEORGE WASHINGTON, *Moral Maxims*

The man who consecrates his hours
By vig'rous effort and an honest aim,
At once he draws the sting of life and death;
He walks with nature; and her paths are peace.

EDWARD YOUNG, *Night Thoughts*

An honest man is respected by all parties.

WILLIAM HAZLITT

It would be an unspeakable advantage, both to the public and private, if men would consider that great truth, that no man is wise or safe but he that is honest.

SIR WALTER RALEIGH

Let honesty be as the breath of thy soul, and never forget to have a penny, when all thy expenses are enumerated and

paid: then shalt thou reach the point of happiness, and independence shall be thy shield and buckler, thy helmet and
crown; then shall thy soul walk upright nor stoop to the
silken wretch because he hath riches, nor pocket an abuse
because the hand which offers it wears a ring set with
diamonds.

BENJAMIN FRANKLIN

There is between my will and all offences
A guard of patience.

SHAKESPEARE, *Troilus and Cressida*

Patience is the best remedy for every trouble.

PLAUTUS, *Rudens*

What cannot be removed, becomes lighter through patience.

HORACE, *Odes*

He that has patience may compass anything.

RABELAIS, *Works*

By patience and time we sever
What strength and rage could never.

JEAN DE LA FONTAINE, *Fables*

Patience is bitter, but its fruit is sweet.

ROUSSEAU, *Émile*

One to whom
Long patience hath such mild composure given,
That patience now doth seem a thing of which
He hath no need.

WILLIAM WORDSWORTH, *Animal Tranquillity and Decay*

Let us run with patience the race that is set before us.

New Testament: Hebrews, XII, 1

Have patience with all things, but chiefly have patience with
yourself. Do not lose courage in considering your own im-
perfections, but instantly set about remedying them—every
day begin the task anew.

ST. FRANCIS DE SALES

Patience for a moment; comfort for ten years.

GREEK PROVERB

Patience is the key to Paradise.

TURKISH PROVERB

Patience is the key of content.

MOHAMMED

Patience and gentleness are power.

LEIGH HUNT

Our real blessings often appear to us in the shape of pains, losses and disappointments; but let us have patience, and we soon shall see them in their proper figures.

JOSEPH ADDISON

Patience; accomplish thy labor; accomplish thy work of affection!
Sorrow and silence are strong, and patient endurance is godlike.
Therefore accomplish thy labor of love, till the heart is made godlike,
Purified, strengthened, perfected, and rendered more worthy of heaven.

LONGFELLOW

The Importance of Good Manners

Manners must adorn knowledge, and smooth its way through the world. Like a great rough diamond, it may do very well in a closet by way of curiosity, and also for its intrinsic value; but it will never be worn, nor shine, if it is not polished.

LORD CHESTERFIELD, *Letters*

Manners are the happy ways of doing things. If they are superficial, so are the dewdrops which give such a depth to the morning meadows.

EMERSON, *Conduct of Life*

Contact with manners is education.

DIONYSIUS OF HALICARNASSUS, *Ars Rhetorica*

The greatest asset that a man or woman or even a child can have is charm. And charm cannot exist without good manners —meaning by this, not so much manners that precisely follow particular rules, as manners that have been made smooth and polished by the continuous practice of kind impulses.

EMILY POST, *Etiquette*

The society of women is the foundation of good manners.

GOETHE, *The Elective Affinities*

For as laws are necessary that good manners may be preserved, so there is need of good manners that laws may be maintained.

MACHIAVELLI, *Dei Discorsi*

Self-respect is at the bottom of all good manners. They are the expression of discipline, of good-will, of respect for other people's rights and comfort and feelings.

EDWARD SANDFORD MARTIN, *A Father to His Freshman Son*

Good manners are the technic of expressing consideration for the feelings of others.

ALICE DUER MILLER, *I Like American Manners*

Manners,—the final and perfect flower of noble character.

WILLIAM WINTER, *The Actor and his Duty*

Men are polished, through act and speech,
  Each by each,
As pebbles are smoothed on the rolling beach.

JOHN TOWNSEND TROWBRIDGE, *A Home Idyl*

Manners make the man.

DANIEL DEFOE, *Complete Gentleman*

The mildest manners, and the gentlest heart.

HOMER, *Iliad*

Teach me, like thee, in various nature wise,
To fall with dignity, with temper rise:
Form'd by thy converse, happily to steer
From grave to gay, from lively to severe;
Correct with spirit, eloquent with ease,
Intent to reason, or polite to please.

ALEXANDER POPE, *Essay on Man*

> True is, that whilom that good poet said,
> The gentle mind by gentle deeds is known;
> For a man by nothing is so well bewray'd
> As by his manners.
> EDMUND SPENSER, *Faerie Queene*

It is good manners which make the excellence of a neighborhood. No wise man will settle where they are lacking.
CONFUCIUS, *Analects*

Manners are of more importance than laws. Upon them, in a great measure, the laws depend. The law touches us but here and there, and now and then. Manners are what vex or soothe, corrupt or purify, exalt or debase, barbarize or refine us, by a constant, steady, uniform, insensible operation, like that of the air we breathe in.
EDMUND BURKE, *Letters on a Regicide Peace*

The manners of every nation are standard of orthodoxy within itself. But these standards being arbitrary, reasonable people in all allow free toleration for the manners, as for the religion, of others.
THOMAS JEFFERSON, *Letter to Jean Baptiste Say*, 1815

Conduct is three-fourths of our life and its largest concern.
MATTHEW ARNOLD, *Literature and Dogma*

Mind and Character

A man's felicity consists not in the outward and visible blessings of fortune, but in the inward and unseen perfections and riches of the mind.

ANACHARSIS

Nothing is at last sacred but the integrity of your own mind.
EMERSON, *Essays*

The mind is the man, and the knowledge of the mind.
BACON

God is Mind, and God is infinite; hence all is Mind.
MARY BAKER EDDY, *Science and Health*

Mind is the great lever of all things.
DANIEL WEBSTER

The mind celebrates a little triumph whenever it can formulate a truth.
SANTAYANA, *The Life of Reason*

One-story intellects, two-story intellects, three-story intellects with skylights. All fact-collectors are one-story men. Two-story men compare, reason, generalize. Three-story men idealize, imagine, predict; their best illumination comes from above, through the skylight.
OLIVER WENDELL HOLMES, *The Poet at the Breakfast Table*

The true, strong, and sound mind is the mind that can embrace equally great things and small.
SAMUEL JOHNSON (Boswell's *Life*)

Strength of mind is exercise, not rest.
POPE, *Essay on Man*

If we work upon marble, it will perish. If we work upon brass, time will efface it. If we rear temples, they will crumble to dust. But if we work upon men's immortal minds, if we imbue them with high principles, with the just fear of God and love of their fellow men, we engrave on those tablets something which no time can efface, and which will brighten and brighten to all eternity.
DANIEL WEBSTER, *Speech*, Faneuil Hall, 1852

A sound mind in a sound body is a thing to be prayed for.
JUVENAL, *Satires*

Talent is nurtured aye in solitude,
But Character 'mid the tempests of the world.
GOETHE, *Torquato Tasso*

Character is like a tree and reputation like its shadow. The shadow is what we think of it; the tree is the real thing.
ABRAHAM LINCOLN

The average mind . . . is charming rather than noble. Had the average mind been noble, we should be completely rational beings without sins or weaknesses or misconduct, and what an insipid world that would be! We should be so much less charming as creatures. I am such a humanist that saints without sins don't interest me.

LIN YUTANG, *The Importance of Living*

Put more trust in nobility of character than in an oath.

SOLON

How can we expect a harvest of thought who have not had a seed-time of character?

THOREAU, *Journal*

His magic was not far to seek—
He was so human! Whether strong or weak,
Far from his kind he neither sank nor soared,
But sate an equal guest at every board:
No beggar ever felt him condescend,
No prince presume; for still himself he bare
At manhood's simple level, and where'er
He met a stranger, there he left a friend.

JAMES RUSSELL LOWELL, *Agassiz*

His daily prayer, far better understood
In acts than words, was simply doing good.

JOHN GREENLEAF WHITTIER, *Daniel Neall*

And, through the heat of conflict, keeps the law
In calmness made, and sees what he foresaw.

WILLIAM WORDSWORTH, *Character of the Happy Warrior*

The secret of the universe, as by slow degrees it reveals itself to us, turns out to be personality.

J. C. POWYS, *The Complex Vision*

Nothing endures but personal qualities.

WALT WHITMAN, *Song of the Broad-Axe*

There is only one way under high Heaven to get anybody do anything—and that is by making the other person want to do it.

DALE CARNEGIE, *How to Win Friends and Influence People*

Behavior, Habit, and Duty

The only guide to a man is his conscience; the only shield to his memory is the rectitude and sincerity of his actions.

WINSTON CHURCHILL

Men's behaviour should be like their apparel, not too strait, or point device, but free for exercise or motion.

BACON, *Essays: Of Ceremonies and Respects*

Man must cease attributing his problems to his environment, and learn again to exercise his will—his personal responsibility in the realm of faith and morals.

ALBERT SCHWEITZER

A beautiful form is better than a beautiful face; a beautiful behavior is better than a beautiful form: it is the finest of the fine arts.

EMERSON, *Essays*

Acting without design, occupying oneself without making a business of it, finding the great in what is small and the many in the few, repaying injury with kindness, effecting difficult things while they are easy, and managing great things in their beginnings: this is the method of Tao.

LAO-TSZE, *The Simple Way*

Be civil to all; sociable to many; familiar with few; friend to one; enemy to none.

BENJAMIN FRANKLIN, *Poor Richard's Almanac*

If not seemly, do it not; if not true, say it not.

MARCUS AURELIUS, Meditations

Love thyself last: cherish those hearts that hate thee:
Corruption wins not more than onesty.
Still in thy right hand carry gentle peace,
To silence envious tongues. Be just, and fear not:
Let all the ends thou aim'st at be thy country's,
Thy God's, and truth's.

SHAKESPEARE, *Henry VIII*

To strive, to seek, to find, and not to yield.

TENNYSON, *Ulysses*

Do all the good you can,
In all the ways you can,
In all the places you can,
At all the times you can,
To all the people you can,
As long as ever you can.

JOHN WESLEY, *Rules of Conduct*

A thought,—good or evil,—an act, in time a habit,—so runs life's law.

RALPH WALDO TRINE, *Life's Law*

Cultivate only the habits that you are willing should master you.

ELBERT HUBBARD, *The Philistine*

A sense of duty is useful in work, but offensive in personal relations.

BERTRAND RUSSELL, *The Conquest of Happiness*

In doing what we ought we deserve no praise, because it is our duty.

ST. AUGUSTINE, *Confessions*

To do my duty in that state of life unto which it shall please God to call me.

Book of Common Prayer: Catechism

No phase of life, whether public or private, can be free from duty.

CICERO, *De Officiis*

So nigh is grandeur to our dust,
So near is God to man,
When Duty whispers low, *Thou must*,
The youth replies, *I can*.

EMERSON, *Voluntaries*

Do well the duty that lies before you.

PITTACUS

Duty then is the sublimest word in our language. Do your duty in all things. You cannot do more. You should never wish to do less.

ROBERT E. LEE

There is no question what the roll of honor in America is. The roll of honor consists of the names of men who have squared their conduct by ideals of duty.

WOODROW WILSON, *Speech*, Washington, Feb. 27, 1916

Living a Full Life

Life's but a means unto an end—that end,
Beginning, mean, and end to all things—God.

PHILIP JAMES BAILEY, *Festus*

A man should share the action and passion of his time at peril of being judged not to have lived.

JUSTICE OLIVER WENDELL HOLMES

Life is a boundless privilege, and when you pay for your ticket, and get into the car, you have no guess what good company you will find there.

RALPH WALDO EMERSON, *Conduct of Life*

The business of life is to go forward.

SAMUEL JOHNSON, *The Idler*

Many people go throughout life committing partial suicide—destroying their talents, energies, creative qualities. Indeed, to learn how to be good to oneself is often more difficult than to learn how to be good to others.

JOSHUA LOTH LIEBMAN, *Peace of Mind*

The secret of life is never to have an emotion that is unbecoming.

> OSCAR WILDE, *A Woman of No Importance*

Life is most enjoy'd,
When courted least; most worth, when disesteem'd.

> EDWARD YOUNG, *Night Thoughts*

As a rule, the game of life is worth playing, but the struggle is the prize.

> DEAN W. R. INGE

Life is a stage, so learn to play your part,
Laying gravity aside, or learn to bear its griefs.

> PALLADAS

One must have lived greatly whose record would bear the full light of day from beginning to its close.

> AMOS BRONSON ALCOTT, *Table Talk: Learning*

Only a life lived for others is a life worth while.

> ALBERT EINSTEIN

Live truly, and thy life shall be
A great and noble creed.

> HORATIUS BONAR, *Be True*

The freer step, the fuller breath,
The wide horizon's grander view,
The sense of life that knows no death—
The life that maketh all things new.

> SAMUEL LONGFELLOW, *The Horizon's View*

Living is an art; and, to practice it well, men need not only acquired skill but also a native tact and taste.

> ALDOUS HUXLEY, *Texts and Pretexts*

To live as fully, as completely as possible, to be happy, and again to be happy is the true aim and end of life.

> LLEWELYN POWYS, *Impassioned Clay*

There are two things to aim at in life: first, to get what you want; and, after that, to enjoy it. Only the wisest of mankind achieve the second.

LOGAN PEARSALL SMITH, *Afterthoughts*

To be honest, to be kind—to earn a little and to spend a little less, to make upon the whole a family happier for his presence, to renounce when that shall be necessary and not be embittered, to keep a few friends but these without capitulation —above all, on the same grim condition to keep friends with himself—here is a task for all that a man has of fortitude and delicacy.

ROBERT LOUIS STEVENSON, *A Christmas Sermon*

But this thing is God, to be man with thy might,
To grow straight in the strength of thy spirit, and live out
thy life as the light.

SWINBURNE, *Hertha*

Where we live or how we live is of little consequence. What is all-important is to live.

ERNEST DIMNET, *What We Live By*

Live to-day, forgetting the anxieties of the past.

EPICURUS

Live all you can; it's a mistake not to. It doesn't so much matter what you do in particular so long as you have your life.

HENRY JAMES, *The Ambassadors*

The whole life of man is but a point of time; let us enjoy it, therefore, while it lasts, and not spend it to no purpose.

PLUTARCH, *Of the Training of Children*

Let us live, then, and be glad,
While young life's before us;
After youthful pastime had,
After old age, hard and sad,
Earth will slumber o'er us.

UNKNOWN, *Gaudeamus Igitur*

A life spent worthily should be measured by a nobler line,—
by deeds, not years.

RICHARD BRINSLEY SHERIDAN, *Pizarro*

Life is long if it is full.

SENECA, *Epistulæ ad Lucilium*

Among good things, I prove and find
The quiet life doth most abound.

JOHN RAY, *English Proverbs*

They may rail at this life—from the hour I began it,
I found it a life full of kindness and bliss;
And until they can show me some happier planet,
More social and bright, I'll content me with this.

THOMAS MOORE, *They May Rail*

From a boy
I gloated on existence. Earth to me
Seemed all-sufficient and my sojourn there
One trembling opportunity for joy.

ALAN SEEGER, *Sonnet: I Loved*

Life is a sweet and joyful thing for one who has some one to
love and a pure conscience.

LEO TOLSTOY, *Two Hussars*

Maturity, we now know, need be no dull routine of a defeated
and resigned adulthood. It can rather be the triumphant use
of powers that all through our childhood and youth have been
in preparation.

HARRY A. OVERSTREET, *The Mature Mind*

Measure of Success

The race is not to the swift, nor the battle to the strong,
neither yet bread to the wise, nor yet riches to men of understanding, nor yet favour to men of skill; but time and chance
happeneth to them all.

Old Testament: Ecclesiastes, IX, 11

The secret of success is constancy to purpose.
BENJAMIN DISRAELI, *Speech*, June 24, 1870

Success is little more than a chemical compound of man with moment.

PHILIP GUEDALLA

In all things, success depends upon previous preparation, and without such preparation there is sure to be failure.

CONFUCIUS, *Analects*

Only he is successful in his business who makes that pursuit which affords him the highest pleasure sustain him.

THOREAU, *Journal*

Nothing succeeds like success.

FRENCH PROVERB

Self-trust is the first secret of success.

EMERSON, *Society and Solitude*

'Tis man's to fight, but Heaven's to give success.

HOMER, *Iliad*

Be studious in your profession, and you will be learned. Be industrious and frugal, and you will be rich. Be sober and temperate, and you will be healthy. Be in general virtuous, and you will be happy. At least, you will, by such conduct, stand the best chance for such consequences.

BENJAMIN FRANKLIN, *Letter to John Alleyn*

All succeeds with people who are sweet and cheerful.

VOLTAIRE, *Le Dépositaire*

To stand upon the ramparts and die for our principles is heroic, but to sally forth to battle and win for our principles is something more than heroic.

FRANKLIN D. ROOSEVELT

Success surely comes with conscience in the long run, other things being equal. Capacity and fidelity are commercially profitable qualities.

HENRY WARD BEECHER

If you wish success in life, make perseverance your bosom friend, experience your wise counselor, caution your elder brother, and hope your guardian genius.

JOSEPH ADDISON

True Happiness

Most folks are about as happy as they make up their minds to be.

ABRAHAM LINCOLN

A happy life must be to a great extent a quiet life, for it is only in an atmosphere of quiet that true joy can live.

BERTRAND RUSSELL, *The Conquest of Happiness*

Just to fill the hour—that is happiness.

EMERSON, *Society and Solitude*

We deem those happy who from the experience of life have learned to bear its ills, without being overcome by them.

JUVENAL, *Satires*

Everybody in the world is seeking happiness—and there is one sure way to find it. That is by controlling your thoughts. Happiness doesn't depend on outward conditions. It depends on inner conditions. It isn't what you have or who you are or where you are or what you are doing that makes you happy or unhappy. It is what you think about it.

DALE CARNEGIE, *How to Win Friends and Influence People*

Happiness lies in the consciousness we have of it, and by no means in the way the future keeps its promises.

GEORGE SAND, *Handsome Lawrence*

The happiness of a man consisteth not in having temporal things in abundance, but a moderate competency sufficeth.

THOMAS à KEMPIS, *De Imitatione Christi*

The happiness of man consists in life, and life is in labor.

LEO TOLSTOY, *What Is to Be Done?*

Nowhere can I think so happily as in a train. I am not inspired; nothing so uncomfortable as that. I am never seized with a sudden plan for a masterpiece, nor form a sudden plan for some new enterprise. My thoughts are just pleasantly reflective. *

A. A. MILNE

There is that in me—I do not know what it is
    —but I know it is in me.
I do not know it—it is without name—it is a word unsaid;
It is not in any dictionary, utterance, symbol.
Something it swings on more than the earth I swing on.
To it the creation is the friend whose embracing awakes me.
It is not chaos or death—it is form, union, plan
    —it is eternal life—it is Happiness.
WALT WHITMAN, *Song of Myself*

How soon a smile of God can change the world!
How we are made for happiness—how work
Grows play, adversity a winning fight!
ROBERT BROWNING, *In a Balcony*

Gladness of the heart is the life of man, and joyfulness of a man prolongeth his days.
Apocrypha: Ecclesiasticus, xxx, 22

The best way to secure future happiness is to be as happy as is rightfully possible to-day.
CHARLES W. ELIOT, *The Happy Life*

Who is the happiest of men? He who values the merits of others,
And in their pleasure takes joy, even as though 'twere his own.
GOETHE, *Distichs*

The happiest people seem to be those who have no particular cause for being happy except that they are so.
DEAN WILLIAM R. INGE

* From *If I May* by A. A. Milne. Published and copyright, 1921, E. P. Dutton & Co., Inc., N. Y. Renewal, 1948, A. A. Milne.

How to gain, how to keep, how to recover happiness is in fact for most men at all times the secret motive of all they do, and of all they are willing to endure.

WILLIAM JAMES, Varieties of Religious Experience

In every part and corner of our life, to lose oneself is to be gainer; to forget oneself is to be happy.

ROBERT LOUIS STEVENSON, Memories and
Portraits: Old Mortality

Happiness grows at our firesides, and is not to be picked in strangers' gardens.

DOUGLAS JERROLD

Happy the man who, unknown to the world, lives content with himself in some retired nook, whom the love of this nothing called fame has never intoxicated with its vain smoke; who makes all his pleasure dependent on his liberty of action, and gives an account of his leisure to no one but himself.

NICOLAS BOILEAU, Épîtres

Peace of mind may transform a cottage into a spacious manor hall; the want of it can make a regal park an imprisoning nutshell.

JOSHUA LOTH LIEBMAN, Peace of Mind

Defining Greatness and Reputation

Greatness is a spiritual condition worthy to excite love, interest, and admiration; and the outward proof of possessing greatness is, that we excite love, interest, and admiration.

MATTHEW ARNOLD, Culture and Anarchy

Greatness, after all, in spite of its name, appears to be not so much a certain size as a certain quality in human lives. It may be present in lives whose range is very small.

PHILLIPS BROOKS, Purpose and Use of Comfort

No great man lives in vain. The History of the world is but the Biography of great men.

THOMAS CARLYLE, Heroes and Hero-Worship

To us he is no more a person
Now, but a whole climate of opinion.
>W. H. AUDEN, *In Memory of Sigmund Freud*

A great man is made up of qualities that meet or make great occasions.
>JAMES RUSSELL LOWELL, *My Study Windows*

The heights by great men reached and kept
Were not attained by sudden flight,
But they, while their companions slept,
Were toiling upward in the night.
>LONGFELLOW, *The Ladder of St. Augustine*

You can't build up a reputation on what you are going to do.
>HENRY FORD

That man is great, and he alone,
Who serves a greatness not his own,
For neither praise nor pelf;
Content to know and be unknown:
Whole in himself.
>OWEN MEREDITH, *A Great Man*

He alone is worthy of the appellation who either does great things, or teaches how they may be done, or describes them with a suitable majesty when they have been done; but those only are great things which tend to render life more happy, which increase the innocent enjoyments and comforts of existence, or which pave the way to a state of future bliss more permanent and more pure.
>JOHN MILTON, *The Second Defence of the People of England*

The greatest truths are the simplest; and so are the greatest men.
>J. C. and A. W. HARE, *Guesses at Truth*

He only is a great man who can neglect the applause of the multitude, and enjoy himself independent of its favour.
>RICHARD STEELE, *The Spectator*

When the high heart we magnify,
    And the clear vision celebrate,
And worship greatness passing by,
    Ourselves are great.
          JOHN DRINKWATER, *Abraham Lincoln*

This be the verse you grave for me:
Here he lies where he longed to be;
Home is the sailor, home from sea,
    And the hunter home from the hill.
          ROBERT LOUIS STEVENSON, *Requiem*.
          (Written for himself,
          and engraved on his tombstone)

Nature never sends a great man into the planet without confiding the secret to another soul.
          RALPH WALDO EMERSON, *Representative Men*

No great intellectual thing was ever done by great effort; a great thing can only be done by a great man, and he does it without effort.
          JOHN RUSKIN, *Pre-Raphaelitism*

Let us say again that the lessons of great men are lost unless they reenforce upon our minds the highest demands which we make upon ourselves; that they are lost unless they drive our sluggish wills forward in the direction of their highest ideals.
          JANE ADDAMS

The invisible thing called a Good Name is made up of the breath of numbers that speak well of you.
          LORD HALIFAX

The only way to compel men to speak good of us is to do it.
          VOLTAIRE

There are two very difficult things in the world. One is to make a name for oneself and the other is to keep it.
          ROBERT SCHUMANN

A good name is rather to be chosen than great riches.
Old Testament: Proverbs, XXXII, 1

Good name in man and woman, dear my lord,
Is the immediate jewel of their souls:
Who steals my purse steals trash; 'tis something, nothing;
'Twas mine, 'tis his, and has been slave to thousands;
But he that filches from me my good name
Robs me of that which not enriches him,
And makes me poor indeed.

SHAKESPEARE, *Othello*

Associate yourself with men of good quality if you esteem your own reputation; for 'tis better to be alone than in bad company.

GEORGE WASHINGTON, *Rules of Civility*

The power of ideals is incalculable. We see no power in a drop of water. But let it get into a crack in the rock and be turned into ice, and it splits the rock; turned into steam, it drives the pistons of the most powerful engines. Something has happened to it which makes active and effective the power that is latent in it.

ALBERT SCHWEITZER

LITERATURE AND ART

The Magic of Books

There is no frigate like a book
To take us lands away,
Nor any coursers like a page
Of prancing poetry.

EMILY DICKINSON, *Poems*

Books have always a secret influence on the understanding;
we cannot at pleasure obliterate ideas: he that reads books
of science, though without any desire fixed of improvement,
will grow more knowing; he that entertains himself with moral
or religious treatises, will imperceptibly advance in goodness;
the ideas which are often offered to the mind, will at last
find a lucky moment when it is disposed to receive them.

SAMUEL JOHNSON, *The Adventurer*

Of all the inanimate objects, of all men's creations, books are
the nearest to us, for they contain our very thoughts, our
ambitions, our indignations, our illusions, our fidelity to truth,
and our persistent leaning toward error. But most of all they
resemble us in their precarious hold on life.

JOSEPH CONRAD, *Notes on Life and Letters*

The images of men's wits and knowledges remain in books;
exempted from the wrong of time, and capable of perpetual
renovation.

FRANCIS BACON, *The Advancement of Learning*

In Books lies the *soul* of the whole Past Time . . . All that
Mankind has done, thought, gained or been: it is lying as in
magic preservation in the pages of Books. They are the chosen
possession of men.

THOMAS CARLYLE, *Heroes and Hero-Worship*

For books are more than books, they are the life
The very heart and core of ages past,
The reason why men lived and worked and died,
The essence and quintessence of their lives.

AMY LOWELL, *The Boston Athenæum*

The first time I read an excellent book, it is to me just as if I had gained a new friend. When I read over a book I have perused before, it resembles the meeting with an old one.
OLIVER GOLDSMITH, *The Citizen of the World*

A book is like a garden carried in the pocket.
ARAB PROVERB

Old wood to burn, old wine to drink, old friends to trust, old books to read.

ALONZO OF ARAGON

A good book is the precious life-blood of a master spirit, embalmed and treasured up on purpose to a Life beyond Life.
JOHN MILTON, *Areopagitica*

Books are the treasured wealth of the world, the fit inheritance of generations and nations.

HENRY DAVID THOREAU, *Walden*

Dreams, books, are each a world; and books, we know,
Are a substantial world, both pure and good:
Round these, with tendrils strong as flesh and blood,
Our pastime and our happiness will grow.
WILLIAM WORDSWORTH, *Personal Talk*

Far more seemly to have thy study full of books, than thy purse full of money.

JOHN LYLY, *Euphues*

Of making many books there is no end.
Old Testament: Ecclesiastes, XII, 12

Even the world itself could not contain the books that should be written.

New Testament: John, XXI, 25

Every age hath its book.

Koran

If a book is worth reading, it is worth buying.
JOHN RUSKIN, *Sesame and Lilies*

When we are collecting books, we are collecting happiness.
VINCENT STARRETT, *The A.B.C. of First Editions*

It is with books as with men: a very small number play a great part, the rest are lost in the multitude.
VOLTAIRE, *Philosophical Dictionary: Books*

If a book comes from the heart, it will contrive to reach other hearts; all art and authorcraft are of small amount to that.
THOMAS CARLYLE, *Heroes and Hero-Worship*

Literature is my Utopia. Here I am not disfranchised. No barrier of the senses shuts me out from the sweet, gracious discourse of my book-friends. They talk to me without embarrassment or awkwardness.
HELEN KELLER, *The Story of My Life*

We are vessels of a very limited content. Not all men can read all books: it is only in a chosen few that any man will find his appointed food.
ROBERT LOUIS STEVENSON, *Books Which Have Influenced Me*

The Artist and His Art

When a work of art appears to be in advance of its period, it is really the period that has lagged behind the work of art.
JEAN COCTEAU

What is art
But life upon the larger scale, the higher,
When, graduating up in a spiral line
Of still expanding and ascending gyres,
It pushes toward the intense significance
Of all things, hungry for the Infinite?
Art's life,—and where we live, we suffer and toil.
ELIZABETH BARRETT BROWNING, *Aurora Leigh*

Art is nothing more than the shadow of humanity.
HENRY JAMES, *Lectures: University in Arts*

All passes. Art alone
    Enduring stays to us:
The Bust outlasts the throne,—
    The Coin, Tiberius.

THÉOPHILE GAUTIER, *L'Art*

Art is simply a right method of doing things. The test of the artist does not lie in the will with which he goes to work, but in the excellence of the work he produces.

THOMAS AQUINAS, *Summa theologiae*

Art is not an end in itself, but a means of addressing humanity.

MOUSSORGSKY

Only the artist, or the free scholar, carries his happiness within him.

BEETHOVEN

Art is a jealous thing; it requires the whole and entire man.

MICHELANGELO

The painter is a painter, because he sees what others only feel or catch a glimpse of, but do not do.

BENEDETTO CROCE, *Aesthetic*

Craftsmanship to be artistic in the final sense must be "loving"; it must care deeply for the subject matter upon which skill is exercised.

JOHN DEWEY, *Art as Experience*

Nature contains the elements, in colour and form, of all pictures, as the keyboard contains the notes of all music. But the artist is born to pick, and choose, and group with science, these elements, that the result may be beautiful.

JAMES MCNEILL WHISTLER

The great artist is the simplifier.

AMIEL, *Journal*

Every artist dips his brush in his own soul, and paints his own nature into his pictures.

HENRY WARD BEECHER

What garlic is to a salad, insanity is to art.

HOMER ST. GAUDENS

> Around the mighty master came
>   The marvels which his pencil wrought,
> Those miracles of power whose fame
>   Is wide as human thought.

JOHN GREENLEAF WHITTIER, *Raphael*

> High is our calling, Friend!—Creative Art
> (Whether the instrument of words she use,
> Or pencil pregnant with ethereal hues,)
> Demands the service of a mind and heart.
> Though sensitive, yet, in their weakest part
> Heroically fashioned.

WILLIAM WORDSWORTH, *Miscellaneous Sonnets*

One picture in ten thousand, perhaps, ought to live in the applause of mankind, from generation to generation until the colors fade and blacken out of sight or the canvas rot entirely away.

NATHANIEL HAWTHORNE, *The Marble Faun*

Every portrait that is painted with feeling is a portrait of the artist, not of the sitter.

OSCAR WILDE, *Picture of Dorian Gray*

Poets and Poetry

> Poets are all who love, who feel great truths,
> And tell them.

PHILIP JAMES BAILEY, *Festus*

> The poet is the truest historian.

JAMES ANTHONY FROUDE, *Homer*

It is a man's sincerity and depth of vision that makes him a poet.

THOMAS CARLYLE, *Heroes and Hero-Worship*

Who writes poetry imbibes honesty from the poisoned lips of life.

WILLIAM ROSE BENÉT, *Man Possessed*

If men will impartially, and not asquint, look toward the offices and function of a poet, they will easily conclude to themselves the impossibility of any man's being a good poet without first being a good man.

BEN JONSON, *Volpone: Dedication*

Who harbors in memory a wealth of valued verse has laid up unto himself treasures that moths will not corrupt nor thieves break in and steal.

JOHN KIERAN

> The world but feels the present's spell,
> The poet feels the past as well;
> Whatever men have done, might do,
> Whatever thought, might think it too.
> MATTHEW ARNOLD, *Bacchanalia*

> A poem should not mean
> But be.
> ARCHIBALD MACLEISH

Poetry atrophies when it gets too far from music.

EZRA POUND

Knowledge of the subject is to the poet what durable materials are to the architect.

SAMUEL JOHNSON

All good poets, epic as well as lyric, compose their beautiful poems not as works of art, but because they are inspired and possessed.

PLATO, *Ion*

To be a poet is to have a soul so quick to discern that no shade of quality escapes it, and so quick to feel that discernment is but a hand playing with finely ordered variety on the chords of emotion: a soul in which knowledge passes instantaneously into feeling, and feeling flashes back as a new organ of knowledge.

GEORGE ELIOT

A great poet is the most precious jewel of a nation.

BEETHOVEN

O divine and mighty power of poetry, thou rescuest all things
from the grasp of death, and biddest the mortal hero live to
all time.

LUCAN, *Pharsalia*

I am nae poet, in a sense,
But just a rhymer like by chance,
An' hae to learning nae pretence;
    Yet, what the matter?
Whene'er my Muse does on me glance,
    I jingle at her.
ROBERT BURNS, *Epistle to John Lapraik*

It is not enough for poems to have beauty; they must have
charm, and lead the hearer's soul where they will.

HORACE, *Ars Poetica*

I would define, in brief, the Poetry of words as the Rhythmical
Creation of Beauty. Its sole arbiter is Taste.

EDGAR ALLAN POE, *The Poetic Principle*

Poetry is the record of the best and happiest moments of the
happiest and best minds.

SHELLEY, *A Defense of Poetry*

The profoundest gift of the spirit of poetry is the gift of
peace.

JOHN COWPER POWYS, *The Meaning of Culture*

I would rather have written that poem, gentlemen, than take
Quebec to-morrow.
MAJOR-GENERAL JAMES WOLFE, (referring to Gray's *Elegy*).
    (Wolfe was killed the following day near Quebec.)

I would rather risk for future fame upon one lyric than upon
ten volumes.

OLIVER WENDELL HOLMES

Your lay, heavenly bard, is to me even as sleep on the grass
to the weary, as in summer heat the slaking of thirst in a
dancing rill of sweet water.

VERGIL, *Eclogues*

Sure, 'tis God's ways is very quare,
    an' far beyont my ken,
How O' the selfsame clay he makes
    Poets an' useful men.
      AGNES KENDRICK GRAY, *The Shepherd to the Poet*

Homer's harp is broken and Horace's lyre is unstrung, and
the voices of the great singers are hushed; but their songs—
their songs are immortal. O friend! what moots it to them
or to us who gave this epic or that lyric to immortality? The
singer belongs to a year, his song to all time.
      EUGENE FIELD, *Love Affairs of a Bibliomaniac*

Verse and nothing else have I to give you.
Other heights in other lives, God willing:
All the gifts from all the heights, your own, Love!
      ROBERT BROWNING, *One Word More*

The poet's eye, in a fine frenzy rolling,
Doth glance from heaven to earth, from earth to heaven;
And as imagination bodies forth
The forms of things unknown, the poet's pen
Turns them to shapes, and gives to airy nothing
A local habitation and a name.
      SHAKESPEARE, *A Midsummer-Night's Dream*

Philosophy and the Search for Wisdom

To be a philosopher is not merely to have subtle thoughts,
nor even to found a school, but so to love wisdom as to live
according to its dictates, a life of simplicity, independence,
magnanimity, and trust.

      THOREAU, *Walden*

The true medicine of the mind is philosophy.
      CICERO, *Tusculanarum Disputationum*

Philosophy is the account which the mind gives to itself of
the constitution of the world.

      EMERSON, *Representative Men*

What I have gained from philosophy is the ability to feel at ease in any society.

ARISTIPPUS

Wisdom is only found in truth.
GOETHE, *Sprüche in Prosa*

The knowledge, *I think, therefore I am*, is the first and most certain that occurs to one who philosophizes orderly.
RENÉ DESCARTES, *Principles of Philosophy*

Wisdom and goodness are twin-born, one heart
Must hold both sisters, never seen apart.
WILLIAM COWPER, *Expostulation*

To finish the moment, to find the journey's end in every step of the road, to live the greatest number of good hours, is wisdom.

EMERSON, *Essays*

The mark of wisdom is to read aright the present, and to march with the occasion.

HOMER

A wise man turns chance into good fortune.
THOMAS FULLER, *Gnomologia*

There is no cure for birth and death save to enjoy the interval.
GEORGE SANTAYANA, *Soliloquies in England*

The greatest good is wisdom.
ST. AUGUSTINE, *Soliloquies*

To exist is to change, to change is to mature.
HENRI BERGSON, *Creative Evolution*

The stream from Wisdom's well,
Which God supplies, is inexhaustible.
BAYARD TAYLOR

Wisdom is the perfect good of the human mind; philosophy is the love of wisdom and the endeavor to attain it.
SENECA, *Epistulæ àd Lucilium*

True wisdom consists not only in seeing what is before your eyes, but in foreseeing what is to come.

TERENCE, Adelphi

> Where is the life we have lost in living?
> Where is the wisdom we have lost in
>   knowledge?
> Where is the knowledge we have lost in
>   information?
> The cycles of Heaven in twenty
>   centuries
> Bring us farther from God and nearer to
>   the Dust.

T. S. ELIOT, The Rock

> It takes a wise man to recognize a wise man.

XENOPHANES

Wisdom is the principal thing; therefore get wisdom: and with all thy getting get understanding.

Old Testament: Proverbs, IV, 7

> Nine-tenths of wisdom is being wise in time.

THEODORE ROOSEVELT, Speech

The Charm of Music

> Music I heard with you was more than music.

CONRAD AIKEN, Music I Heard With You

> There is no truer truth obtainable
> By Man than comes of music.

ROBERT BROWNING, Parleyings with Certain People

> Music resembles poetry; in each
> Are nameless graces which no methods teach,
> And which a master-hand alone can reach.

POPE, Essay on Criticism

Drum on your drums, batter on your banjos,
   sob on the long cool winding saxophones.
   Go to it, O jazzmen.
Sling your knuckles on the bottoms of the
   happy tin pans, let your trombones ooze,
   and go husha-husha-hush with the
   slippery sandpaper.
               CARL SANDBURG, *Jazz Fantasia*

Music hath charms to soothe the savage beast,
To soften rocks, or bend a knotted oak.
        WILLIAM CONGREVE, *The Mourning Bride*

For Orpheus' lute was strung with poets' sinews,
Whose golden touch could soften steel and stones,
Make tigers tame and huge leviathans
Forsake unbounded deeps to dance on sands.
     SHAKESPEARE, *The Two Gentlemen of Verona*

Music can only be really alive when there are listeners who
are really alive. To listen intently, to listen consciously, to
listen with one's whole intelligence is the least we can do
in the furtherance of an art that is one of the glories of
mankind.
      AARON COPLAND, *What to Listen for in Music*

Commemoration-mad; content to hear
(Oh wonderful effect of music's pow'r!)
Messiah's eulogy, for Handel's sake.
            WILLIAM COWPER, *The Task*

"This is the way," laughed the great god Pan
   (Laughed while he sat by the river),
"The only way since gods began
To make sweet music, they could succeed."
Then, dropping his mouth to a hole in the reed,
   He blew in power by the river.
       E. B. BROWNING, *A Musical Instrument*

Sweetest melodies
Are those that are by distance made more sweet.
         WORDSWORTH, *Personal Talk*

Heard melodies are sweet, but those unheard
    Are sweeter; therefore, ye soft pipes, play on;
Not to the sensual ear, but, more endear'd,
    Pipe to the spirit ditties of no tone.
KEATS, Ode on a Grecian Urn

I pant for the music which is divine;
    My heart in its thirst is a dying flower;
Pour forth the sound like enchanted wine,
    Loosen the notes in a silver shower;
Like a herbless plain, for the gentle rain,
    I gasp, I faint, till they wake again.
SHELLEY, Music

There is sweet music here that softer falls
Than petals from blown roses on the grass,
Music that gentlier on the spirit lies,
Than tired eyelids upon tired eyes;
Music that brings sweet sleep down from the blissful skies.
TENNYSON, The Lotos-Eaters: Choric Song

There's music in the sighing of a reed;
    There's music in the gushing of a rill;
    There's music in all things, if men had ears:
    Their earth is but an echo of the spheres.
BYRON, Don Juan

A velvet flute-note fell down pleasantly
Upon the bosom of that harmony,
Somewhat, half song, half odor, forth did float
As if a rose might somehow be a throat.
SIDNEY LANIER, The Symphony

The language of tones belongs equally to all mankind, and
melody is the absolute language in which the musician speaks
to every heart.
RICHARD WAGNER, Beethoven

There's a barrel-organ carolling across a golden street
    In the city as the sun sinks low;
And the music's not immortal; but the world has made it sweet
    And fulfilled it with the sunset glow.
ALFRED NOYES, The Barrel-Organ

My mother used to say that a hearing of Bach's *Chaconne* always reminded her of the Sermon on the Mount, and that the introduction of the major variations represented the Beatitudes.

ALBERT SPALDING, *Rise to Follow*

Beauty

Beauty is not caused,
It is.

EMILY DICKINSON, *Further Poems*

Beauty is heaven's gift, and how few can boast of beauty!

OVID, *The Art of Love*

The best part of beauty is that which a picture cannot express.

BACON, *Apothegms*

For beauty being the best of all we know
Sums up the unsearchable and secret aims
Of nature.

ROBERT BRIDGES, *The Growth of Love*

Wisdom is the abstract of the past, but beauty is the promise of the future.

OLIVER WENDELL HOLMES, *The Professor at the Breakfast-Table*

Beauty is something wonderful and strange that the artist fashions out of the chaos of the world in the torment of his soul.

W. SOMERSET MAUGHAM, *The Moon and Sixpence*

Beauty is a form of genius—is higher, indeed, than Genius, as it needs no explanation.

OSCAR WILDE, *The Picture of Dorian Gray*

No spring nor summer beauty hath such grace
As I have seen in one autumnal face.

JOHN DONNE, *Elegy IX*

The beautiful is as useful as the useful,
and sometimes more so.
>   MATILDA BETHAM-EDWARDS, *French Fireside Poetry*

Who walks with Beauty has no need of fear;
The sun and moon and stars keep pace with him,
Invisible hands restore the ruined year,
And time, itself, grows beautifully dim.
>   DAVID MORTON, *Who Walks With Beauty*

Spirit of Beauty, whose sweet impulses,
Flung like the rose of dawn across the sea,
Alone can flush the exalted consciousness
With shafts of sensible divinity—
Light of the world, essential to loveliness.
>   ALAN SEEGER, *Ode to Natural Beauty*

Doth perfect beauty stand in need of praise? Nay; no more
than law, no more than truth, no more than loving kindness,
nor than modesty.

>   MARCUS AURELIUS, *Meditations*

Physical beauty is the sign of an interior beauty, a spiritual and
moral beauty which is the basis, the principle, and the unity of
the beautiful.
>   SCHILLER, *Essays, Esthetical and Philosophical*

If I were called upon to choose between beauty and truth, I
should not hesitate; I should hold to beauty, being confident
that it bears within it a truth both higher and deeper than truth
itself. I will go so far as to say there is nothing true in the
world save beauty.

>   ANATOLE FRANCE

Goodness is a special kind of truth and beauty. It is truth and
beauty in human behavior.
>   H. A. OVERSTREET, *The Enduring Quest*

A thing of beauty is a joy for ever:
Its loveliness increases; it will never
Pass into nothingness; but still will keep
A bower quiet for us, and a sleep
Full of sweet dreams, and health, and quiet breathing.
>   KEATS, *Endymion*

She walks in beauty, like the night
Of cloudless climes and starry skies;
And all that's best of dark and bright
Meet in her aspect and her eyes:
Thus mellow'd to that tender light
Which heaven to gaudy day denies.

                    BYRON, *She Walks in Beauty*

The most beautiful object in the world, it will be allowed, is a beautiful woman.

                                        MACAULAY

Knowledge and Learning

An investment in knowledge pays the best interest.

        BENJAMIN FRANKLIN, *Poor Richard's Almanac*

All our progress is an unfolding, like the vegetable bud.
You have first an instinct, then an opinion, then a knowledge.

                                EMERSON, *Essays*

Knowledge and timber shouldn't be much used till they are seasoned.

        OLIVER WENDELL HOLMES, *The Autocrat of the
                                Breakfast-Table*

Let knowledge grow from more to more,
But more of reverence in us dwell;
That mind and soul, according well,
May make one music as before.

                        TENNYSON, *In Memoriam*

Knowledge is the only fountain, both of the love and the principles of human liberty.

                                DANIEL WEBSTER

The fundamental cause of trouble in the world today is that the stupid are cocksure while the intelligent are full of doubt.

                                BERTRAND RUSSELL

It is far better to know something about everything than to know all about one thing. Universality is the best.

PASCAL, *Pensées*

The knowledge of man is as the waters, some descending from above, and some springing up from beneath; the one informed by the light of nature, the other inspired by divine revelation.

BACON, *The Advancement of Learning*

O what a brave thing it is, in every case and circumstance of a matter, to be thoroughly well informed!

RABELAIS, *Works*

Nothing is so firmly believed as what we least know.

MONTAIGNE

Every addition to true knowledge is an addition to human power.

HORACE MANN, *Lectures on Education*

A wise man is strong; yea, a man of knowledge increaseth strength.

Old Testament: Proverbs, XXIV, 5

Deign on the passing world to turn thine eyes,
And pause awhile from letters, to be wise.

SAMUEL JOHNSON, *The Vanity of Human Wishes*

All I know is what I read in the papers.

WILL ROGERS

When you know a thing, to hold that you know it; and when you do not know a thing, to allow that you do not know it: this is knowledge.

CONFUCIUS, *Analects*

Wear your learning like your watch, in a private pocket; and do not pull it out, and strike it, merely to show that you have one.

LORD CHESTERFIELD

As a field, however fertile, cannot be fruitful without cultivation, neither can a mind without learning.

CICERO, *Tusculanarum Disputationum*

Learning is ever in the freshness of its youth, even for the old.

AESCHYLUS, *Agamemnon*

I grow old learning something new every day.

SOLON

Words and Their Power

All words are pegs to hang ideas on.

HENRY WARD BEECHER

To a man of understanding only a word is necessary.

RABELAIS, *Works*

The art of words is the culmination of artistic creation.

OTTO RANK, *Art and Artist*

But words are things; and a small drop of ink,
Falling, like dew, upon a thought, produces
That which makes thousands, perhaps millions, think.

BYRON, *Don Juan*

Word by word the book is made.

French Proverb

How strong an influence works in well-placed words.

GEORGE CHAPMAN, *The Gentleman Usher*

Without knowing the force of words, it is impossible to know men.

CONFUCIUS, *Analects*

Heaven and earth shall pass away, but my words shall not pass away.

New Testament: Matthew, XXIV, 35

A word spoken in due season, how good is it!
Old Testament: Proverbs, xv, 23

Loyal words have the secret of healing grief.
MENANDER, *Fragments*

I love smooth words, like gold-enameled fish
Which circle slowly with a silken swish,
And tender ones, like downy-feathered birds:
Words shy and dappled, deep-eyed deer in herds.
ELINOR WYLIE, *Pretty Words*

Kind words are benedictions.
FREDERICK SAUNDERS, *Stray Leaves*

In words as fashions the same rule will hold,
Alike fantastic if too new or old:
Be not the first by whom the new are tried,
Nor yet the last to lay the old aside.
POPE, *Essay on Criticism*

Clearness is the most important matter in the use of words.
QUINTILIAN, *De Institutione Oratoria*

Few words, but proceeding from a heart filled with truth.
LUCAN, *De Bello Civili*

Words, like fine flowers, have their colours too.
ERNEST RHYS, *Words*

My words are little jars
For you to take and put upon a shelf.
Their shapes are quaint and beautiful,
And they have many pleasant colours and lustres
To recommend them.
Also the scent from them fills the room
With sweetness of flowers and crushed grasses.
AMY LOWELL, *A Gift*

Look out how you use proud words.
When you let proud words go, it is not easy to call them back.
CARL SANDBERG, *Primer Lesson*

The wise Plato saith, as ye may read,
The word must needs accorde with the deed.
                    CHAUCER, *Maunciples Tale*

God blesses still the generous thought,
    And still the fitting word He speeds,
And Truth, at His requiring taught,
    He quickens into deeds.
                    JOHN GREENLEAF WHITTIER, *Channing*

To honour his own word as if his God's.
                    TENNYSON, *Guinevere*

Language is the only instrument of science, and words are but
the signs of ideas.
    SAMUEL JOHNSON, (from the Preface to his Dictionary)

Language, as well as the faculty of speech, was the immediate
gift of God.
    NOAH WEBSTER, (from the Preface to his Dictionary)

To be able to read and to write, is to learn to profit by and
to partake of the greatest of human achievements, that which
makes all other human achievements possible: namely the
pooling of knowledge and experience into a great co-operative
store of life information, available (except where censorship
or suppression prevent it) to all.
    S. I. HAYAKAWA, *Language in Action*

Good Writing

I think it will be found that the grand style arises in poetry
when a noble nature, poetically gifted, treats with simplicity
or with severity a serious subject.
                    MATTHEW ARNOLD

A poet does not work by square or line.
                    WILLIAM COWPER, *Conversation*

There are nine and sixty ways of constructing tribal lays,
And—every—single—one—of—them—is—right!
                    RUDYARD KIPLING, *In the Neolithic Age*

gods i am pent in a cockroach
i with the soul of a dante
am mate and companion of fleas
i with the gift of a homer
must smile when a mouse calls me pal
tumble bugs are my familiars
this is the punishment meted
because i have written vers libre

DON MARQUIS, *the wail of archy*

Writing free verse is like playing tennis with the net down.

ROBERT FROST, *Address*

I always make the first verse well, but I have trouble in making the others.

MOLIÈRE, *Les Précieuses Ridicules*

I wish our clever young poets would remember my homely definitions of prose and poetry; that is, prose—words in their best order; poetry,—the best words in their best order.

SAMUEL TAYLOR COLERIDGE, *Table Talk*

One merit of poetry few persons will deny: it says more and in fewer words than prose.

VOLTAIRE, *A Philosophical Dictionary: Poets*

The greatest part of a writer's time is spent in reading, in order to write; a man will turn over half a library to make one book.

SAMUEL JOHNSON, (Boswell's *Life*)

Knowledge is the foundation and source of good writing.

HORACE, *Ars Poetica*

While writing the very toil gives pleasure, and the growing work glows with the writer's heart.

OVID, *Epistulæ ex Ponto*

Whate'er is well-conceived is clearly said,
And the words to say it flow with ease.

NICHOLAS BOILEAU, *L'Art Poétique*

True ease in writing comes from art not chance.

ALEXANDER POPE, *Essay on Criticism*

Ready writing makes not good writing; but good writing brings
on ready writing.

BEN JONSON

To be a well-favoured man is a gift of fortune: but to write
and read comes by nature.

SHAKESPEARE, *Much Ado About Nothing*

The Theatre

The play's the thing.

SHAKESPEARE, *Hamlet*

In all ages the drama, through its portrayal of the acting and
suffering spirit of man, has been more closely allied than any
other art to his deeper thoughts concerning his nature and his
destiny.

LUDWIG LEWISOHN, *The Modern Drama*

There is a mode in plays as well as clothes.

JOHN DRYDEN, *Rival Ladies: Prologue*

If you fashion a fresh character, have it kept to the end as
it was in the beginning, consistent with itself.

HORACE, *Ars Poetica*

The first Act's doubtful, but we say
It is the last commends the Play.

ROBERT HERRICK, *The Plaudite*

Your true right tragedy is enacted on the stage of a man's soul,
and with the man's reason as lone auditor.

JAMES BRANCH CABELL, *Cream of the Jest*

The theatre is no place for painful speculation; it is a place
for diverting representation.

H. L. MENKEN, *Prejudices*, Series one

The aim and perhaps the mission of drama are simply, through
the instrumentality of art, to give platitudes a fresh breath of
life and now and then, where possible, overtones of beauty.

GEORGE JEAN NATHAN, *Art of the Night*

"Do you come to the play without knowing what it is?" "O, yes, Sir, yes, very frequently. I have no time to read play-bills. One merely comes to meet one's friends, and show that one's alive."

FANNY BURNEY, Evelina

> The stage but echoes back the public voice;
> The drama's laws, the drama's patrons give,
> For we that live to please, must please to live.

SAMUEL JOHNSON, Prologue at the Opening
of the Drury Lane Theatre

An actor is a sculptor who carves in snow.

LAWRENCE BARRETT

To see Kean act was like reading Shakespeare by flashes of lightning.

COLERIDGE, Table Talk

> And on the last day when we leave those we love
> And move in a mournful procession,
> I hope we'll both play star engagements above,
> For I'm sure they "admit the profession."

JOSEPH JEFFERSON, Letter, to Laurence Hutton

> The play is done; the curtain drops,
>   Slow falling to the prompter's bell:
> A moment yet the actor stops,
>   And looks around, to say farewell.
> It is an irksome word and task:
>   And, when he's laughed and said his say,
> He shows, as he removes the mask,
>   A face that's anything but gay.

WILLIAM MAKEPEACE THACKERAY, The End of the Play

Come, children, let us shut up the box and the puppets, for our play is played out.

THACKERAY, Vanity Fair

> What would he do,
> Had he the motive and the cue for passion
> That I have? He would drown the stage with tears.

SHAKESPEARE, Hamlet

Never meddle with actors, for they are a favored class.
CERVANTES, *Don Quixote*

Then there are the precious few, standing at the top of their profession, whose high gift it is to act themselves, to adopt their spirits to the spirits of the parts they are playing, to possess and then to be possessed by the characters they project, and to give them the benefit of their beauty, and their intelligence, their sympathy and their virtuosity, their poetry and their inner radiance, their imagination and their glamour.
JOHN MASON BROWN, *The Art of Playgoing*

NATURE

The Seasons

Therefore all seasons shall be sweet to thee,
Whether the summer clothe the general earth
With greenness, or the redbreast sit and sing
Betwixt the tufts of snow on the bare branch
Of mossy apple-tree.
> SAMUEL TAYLOR COLERIDGE, *Frost at Midnight*

Sing a song of seasons!
Something bright in all!
Flowers in the summer,
Fires in the fall.
> ROBERT LOUIS STEVENSON, *Autumn Fires*

January snowy; February flowy; March blowy.
April show'ry; May flow'ry; June bow'ry.
July moppy; August croppy; September poppy.
October breezy; November wheezy; December freezy.
> RICHARD BRINSLEY SHERIDAN, *The Calendar*

The year's at the spring
And day's at the morn;
Morning's at seven;
The hill-side's dew-pearled;
The lark's on the wing;
The snail's on the thorn;
God's in his heaven——
All's right with the world!
> ROBERT BROWNING, *Pippa Passes*

The season pricketh every gentle heart,
And maketh him out of his sleep to start.
> CHAUCER, *The Knightes Tale*

When the trellised grapes their flowers unmask,
And the new-born tendrils twine,
The old wine darkling in the cask
Feels the bloom on the living vine,
And burst the hoops at hint of spring.
> RALPH WALDO EMERSON, *May-Day*

> The Spring's already at the gate
>   With looks my care beguiling;
> The country round appeareth straight
>   A flower-garden smiling.
>
> > HEINRICH HEINE, *Books of Songs*

> Every clod feels a stir of might,
>   An instinct within it that reaches and towers
> And, groping blindly above it for light,
>   Climbs to a soul in grass and flowers.
>
> > JAMES RUSSELL LOWELL, *The Vision of Sir Launfal*

> Spring rides no horses down the hill,
> But comes on foot, a goose-girl still.
> And all the loveliest things there be
> Come simply so, it seems to me.
>
> > EDNA ST. VINCENT MILLAY, *The Goose-Girl*

For, lo, the winter is past, the rain is over and gone; the flowers appear on the earth; the time of the singing of birds is come, and the voice of the turtle is heard in our land.

> *Old Testament: Song of Solomon*, II, 11, 12

So does our spring begin, in a slow flowering on the leafless wood of the bough of hazel and alder and poplar and willow, a hardy business, a spawning upon the air, like the spawning in the ponds, a flowering so primitive that it carries us back to ancient geologic times, when trees that are now fossils sowed the wind like these, their descendants—an epoch when the world, too, was in its naked springtime.

> DONALD CULROSS PEATTIE, *An Almanac for Moderns*

> When the hounds of spring are on winter's traces,
>   The mother of months in meadow or plain
> Fills the shadows and windy places
>   With lisp of leaves and ripple of rain.
>
> > SWINBURNE, *Atalanta in Calydon: Chorus*

> In spring time, the only pretty ring time,
> When birds do sing, hey ding a ding, ding:
> Sweet lovers love the spring.
>
> > SHAKESPEARE, *As You Like It*

There is something of summer in the hum of insects.
    WALTER SAVAGE LANDOR, *Letter to Southey*

    Now simmer blinks on flowery braes,
    And o'er the crystal streamlet plays.
        ROBERT BURNS, *The Birks of Aberfeldy*

    Then came the jolly Summer, being dight
    In a thin silken cassock, coloured green,
    That was unlinèd all, to be more light.
        EDMUND SPENSER, *Faerie Queene*

    How bravely Autumn paints upon the sky
    The gorgeous fame of Summer which is fled!
    THOMAS HOOD, *Written in a Volume of Shakespeare*

O Autumn, laden with fruit, and stainèd
With the blood of the grape, pass not, but sit
Beneath my shady roof; there thou may'st rest
And tune thy jolly voice to my fresh pipe,
And all the daughters of the year shall dance!
Sing now the lusty song of fruits and flowers.
        WILLIAM BLAKE, *To Autumn*

        The red upon the hill
        Taketh away my will;
        If anybody sneer,
        Take care, for God is here,
        That's all.
        EMILY DICKINSON, *Mysteries*

    Season of mists and mellow fruitfulness.
        JOHN KEATS, *To Autumn*

It was Autumn, and incessant
    Piped the quails from shocks and sheaves,
And, like living coals, the apples
    Burned among the withering leaves.
        LONGFELLOW, *Pegasus in Pound*

O, it sets my heart a clickin' like the tickin' of a clock,
When the frost is on the punkin and the fodder's in the shock.
JAMES WHITCOMB RILEY, *When the Frost is on the Punkin*

The tints of autumn—a mighty flower garden blossoming under the spell of the enchanter, Frost.

JOHN GREENLEAF WHITTIER, *Patucket Falls*

My sorrow when she's here with me,
    Thinks these dark days of autumn rain
Are beautiful as days can be;
She loves the bare, the withered tree;
    She walks the sodden pasture lane.

ROBERT FROST, *My November Guest*

O Winter, ruler of th' inverted year,
I crown thee king of intimate delights,
Fire-side enjoyments, home-born happiness,
And all the comforts that the lowly roof
Of undisturb'd retirement, and the hours
Of long uninterrupted ev'ning, know.

WILLIAM COWPER, *The Task*

Late February days; and now, at last,
Might you have thought that Winter's woe was past;
So fair the sky was and so soft the air.

WILLIAM MORRIS, *The Earthly Paradise: February*

If Winter comes, can Spring be far behind?

SHELLEY, *Ode to the West Wind*

Such a winter eve. Now for a mellow fire, some old poet's page, or else serene philosophy.

HENRY DAVID THOREAU, *Journal*

Joy in Nature

By fate, not option, frugal Nature gave
One scent to hyson and to wall-flower,
One sound to pine-groves and to waterfalls,
One aspect to the desert and the lake.
It was her stern necessity.

EMERSON, *Xenophanes*

And what if all of animated nature
Be but organic harps diversely fram'd,
That tremble into thought, as o'er them sweeps,
Plastic and vast, one intellectual breeze,
At once the soul of each, and God of all?
COLERIDGE, *The Eolian Harp*

Meanwhile, until the world's structure is held together by
philosophy, she [nature] maintains its working through hunger
and through love.

SCHILLER, *Die Weltweisen*

Nature will bear the closest inspection. She invites us to lay
our eye level with her smallest leaf, and take an insect view
of its plain.

THOREAU, *Journal*

About nature consult nature herself.
BACON, *De Augmentis Scientiarum*

Nature does nothing in vain.
SIR THOMAS BROWNE, *Religio Medici*

No tears
Dim the sweet look that Nature wears.
LONGFELLOW, *Sunrise on the Hills*

The saddest heart might pleasure take
To see all nature gay.
SIR WALTER SCOTT, *Marmion*

To be beautiful and to be calm is the ideal of nature.
RICHARD JEFFERIES, *The Pageant of Summer*

All that thy seasons bring, O Nature, is fruit for me!
All things come from thee, subsist in thee, go back to thee.
MARCUS AURELIUS, *Meditations*

There is a pleasure in the pathless woods,
There is a rapture on the lonely shore,
There is society where none intrudes,
By the deep Sea, and music in its roar;
I love not Man the less, but Nature more,

From these our interviews, in which I steal
From all I may be, or have been before,
To mingle with the Universe, and feel
What I can ne'er express, yet cannot all conceal.
                    BYRON, *Childe Harold*

          The sounding cataract
Haunted me like a passion: the tall rock,
The mountain, and the deep and gloomy wood,
Their colours and their forms, were then to me
An appetite; a feeling and a love,
That had no need of a remoter charm,
By thought supplied.
    WORDSWORTH, *Lines Composed a Few Miles Above
                            Tintern Abbey*

Yet nature's charms—the hills and woods—
The sweeping vales and foaming floods—
    Are free alike to all.
                    ROBERT BURNS, *To Chloris*

Nature's great law, and law of all men's minds?—
To its own impulse every creature stirs;
Live by thy light, and earth will live by hers!
            MATTHEW ARNOLD, *Religious Isolation*

The study of Nature is intercourse with the Highest Mind.
        JEAN LOUIS AGASSIZ, *Agassiz at Penikese*

Go, from the creatures thy instructions take:
Learn from the birds what food the thickets yield;
Learn from the beasts the physic of the field;
Thy arts of building from the bee receive;
Learn of the mole to plough, the worm to weave;
Learn of the little nautilus to sail,
Spread the thin oar, and catch the driving gale.
                    POPE, *Essay on Man*

And this our life, exempt from public haunt
Finds tongues in trees, books in the running brooks,
Sermons in stones, and good in every thing.
                SHAKESPEARE, *As You Like It*

    Nature is the art of God.
                    DANTE, *De Monarchia*

Trees

At the gates of the forest, the surprised man of the world is forced to leave his city estimates of great and small, wise and foolish. The knapsack of custom falls off his back.

EMERSON, *Essays*

To linger silent among the healthful woods, musing on such things as are worthy of a wise and good man.

HORACE, *Epistles*

The forests of America, however slighted by man, must have been a great delight to God; for they were the best he ever planted.

JOHN MUIR, *The American Forests*

Among the scenes which are deeply impressed on my mind, none exceed in sublimity the primeval forests undefaced by the hand of man. No one can stand in these solitudes unmoved, and not feel that there is more in man than the mere breath of his body.

CHARLES DARWIN, *Journal during the Voyage of H.M.S. Beagle*

The woods please us above all things.

VERGIL, *Eclogues*

I like trees because they seem more resigned to the way they have to live than other things do.

WILLA CATHER, *O Pioneers*

One impulse from a vernal wood
May teach you more of man,
Of moral evil and of good,
Than all the sages can.

WORDSWORTH, *The Tables Turned*

What plant we in this apple-tree?
Buds, which the breath of summer days
Shall lengthen into leafy sprays;
Boughs where the thrush, with crimson breast,

Shall haunt, and sing, and hide her nest;
    We plant, upon the sunny lea,
A shadow for the noontide hour,
A shelter from the summer shower,
    When we plant the apple-tree.
WILLIAM CULLEN BRYANT, *The Planting of the Apple-Tree*

        I'll lie here and learn
        How, over their ground,
        Trees make a long shadow
        And a light sound.
            LOUISE BOGAN, *Knowledge*

He that planteth a tree is the servant of God,
He provideth a kindness for many generations,
And faces that he hath not seen shall bless him.
        HENRY VAN DYKE, *The Friendly Trees*

The very leaves live for love and in his season every happy
tree experiences love's power.
        CLAUDIAN, *De Nuptiis Honorii Augusti*

        I think that I shall never see
        A poem lovely as a tree.
            JOYCE KILMER, *Trees*

    Cedar, and pine, and fir, and branching palm,
    A sylvan scene, and as the ranks ascend
    Shade above shade, a woody theatre
    Of stateliest view.
            MILTON, *Paradise Lost*

    Under the greenwood tree
    Who loves to lie with me,
    And tune his merry note
    Unto the sweet bird's throat,
    Come hither, come hither, come hither:
    Here shall he see
    No enemy
    But winter and rough weather.
            SHAKESPEARE, *As You Like It*

Much can they praise the trees so straight and high,
The sailing pine, the cedar proud and tall,
The vine-prop elm, the poplar never dry,
The builder oak, sole king of forests all,
The aspen good for staves, the cypress funeral,
The laurel, meed of mighty conquerors
And poets sage, the fir that weepest still,
The willow worn of forlorn paramours,
The yew obedient to the bender's will,
The birch for shafts, the sallow for the mill,
The myrrh sweet-bleeding in the bitter wound,
The warlike beech, the ash for nothing ill,
The fruitful olive, and the platane round,
The carver holme, the maple seldom inward sound.
EDMUND SPENSER, *Faerie Queene*

I think that I shall never see
A billboard lovely as a tree.
Perhaps, unless the billboards fall,
I'll never see a tree at all.
OGDEN NASH, *Song of the Open Road*

Loveliest of trees, the cherry now
Is hung with bloom along the bough,
And stands about the woodland ride
Wearing white for Eastertide.
A. E. HOUSMAN, *A Shropshire Lad*

The chestnut's proud, and the lilac's pretty,
The poplar's gentle and tall,
But the plane tree's kind to the poor dull city—
I love him best of all!
EDITH NESBIT, *Child's Song in Spring*

Like two cathedral towers these stately pines
Uplift their fretted summits tipped with cones;
The arch beneath them is not built with stones,
Not Art but Nature traced these lovely lines,
And carved this graceful arabesque of vines;
No organ but the wind here sighs and moans,
No sepulchre conceals a martyr's bones,
No marble bishop on his tomb reclines.

Enter! the pavement, carpeted with leaves,
Gives back a softened echo to thy tread!
Listen! the choir is singing; all the birds,
In leafy galleries beneath the eaves,
Are singing! listen, ere the sound be fled,
And learn there may be worship without words.
                    LONGFELLOW, *My Cathedral*

O Reader! hast thou ever stood to see
        The Holly Tree?
The eye that contemplates it well perceives
        Its glossy leaves
Order'd by an intelligence so wise
As might confound the Atheist's sophistries.
                    SOUTHEY, *The Holly Tree*

Except during the nine months before he draws his first
breath, no man manages his affairs as well as a tree does.
                    G. B. SHAW

God wrote his loveliest poem on the day
He made the first tall silver poplar tree.
                    GRACE NOLL CROWELL, *Silver Poplars*

The talking oak
To the ancient spoke.
But any tree
Will talk to me.
        MARY CAROLYN DAVIES, *Be Different to Trees*

Ancient Pines,
Ye bear no record of the years of man.
Spring is your sole historian.
        BAYARD TAYLOR, *The Pine Forest of Monterey*

Birds

The little birds of the field have God for their caterer.
                    CERVANTES, *Don Quixote*

Be like the bird which on frail branches balanced
    A moment sits and sings;
He feels them tremble, but he sings unshaken,
    Knowing that he has wings.

                    Victor Hugo, *Wings*

Then from the neighboring thicket the mocking-bird,
    wildest of singers,
Swinging aloft on a willow spray that hung o'er the water,
Shook from his little throat such floods of delirious music,
That the whole air and the woods and the waves seemed
    silent to listen.

                  Longfellow, *Evangeline*

I value my garden more for being full of blackbirds than of
cherries, and very frankly give them fruit for their songs.
                  Joseph Addison, *The Spectator*

At once a voice arose among
    The bleak twigs overhead
In a full-hearted evensong
    Of joy illimited;
An aged thrush, frail, gaunt, and small,
    In blast-beruffled plume,
Had chosen thus to fling his soul
    Upon the growing gloom.
So little cause for carolings
    Of such ecstatic sound
Was written on terrestrial things
    Afar or nigh around,
That I could think there trembled through
    His happy good-night air
Some blessed Hope, whereof he knew
    And I was unaware.

                Thomas Hardy, *The Darkling Thrush*

The nightingale has a lyre of gold,
    The lark's is a clarion call,
And the blackbird plays but a boxwood flute,
    But I love him best of all.

                William Ernest Henley, *Echoes*

The birds have ceased their songs,
All save the blackbird, that from yon tall ash,
In adoration of the setting sun,
Chants forth his evening hymn.

DAVID MOIR, *An Evening Sketch*

Near all the birds
Will sing at dawn—and yet we do not take
The chaffering swallow for the holy lark.

E. B. BROWNING, *Aurora Leigh*

Hark, hark! the lark at heaven's gate sings,
And Phœbus 'gins arise.

SHAKESPEARE, *Cymbeline*

But the Lark is so brimful of gladness and love,
The green fields below him, the blue sky above,
That he sings, and he sings, and for ever sings he—
"I love my Love, and my Love loves me!"

COLERIDGE, *Answer to a Child's Question*

To hear the lark begin his flight
And singing, startle the dull night,
From his watch-tower in the skies,
Till the dappled Dawn doth rise;
Then to come, in spite of sorrow,
And at my window bid good morrow.

MILTON, *L'Allegro*

Hail to thee, blithe Spirit!—
Bird thou never wert!—
That from Heaven, or near it,
Pourest thy full heart
In profuse strains of unpremeditated art.

SHELLEY, *To a Skylark*

Leave to the nightingale her shady wood;
A privacy of glorious light is thine:
Whence thou dost pour upon the world a flood
Of harmony, with instinct more divine:
Type of the wise who soar, but never roam:
True to the kindred points of Heaven and Home!

WORDSWORTH, *To a Skylark*

Thou wast not born for death, immortal Bird!
    No hungry generations tread thee down;
The voice I hear this passing night was heard
    In ancient days by emperor and clown:
Perhaps the self-same song that found a path
    Through the sad heart of Ruth, when, sick for home,
She stood in tears amid the alien corn;
    The same that oft-times hath
Charm'd magic casements, opening on the foam
Of perilous seas, in faery lands forlorn.
                 KEATS, *Ode to a Nightingale*

I had a silvery name, I had a silvery name,
I had a silvery name—do you remember
The name you cried beside the tumbling sea?
"Darling—darling—darling—darling—"
Said the Chinese nightingale.
        VACHEL LINDSAY, *The Chinese Nightingale*

Yon nightingale, whose strain so sweetly flows,
    Mourning her ravish'd young or much-loved mate,
A soothing charm o'er all the valleys throws
    And skies, with notes well tuned to her sad state.
             PETRARCH, *To Laura in Death*

The sunrise wakes the lark to sing,
    The moonrise wakes the nightingale.
Come, darkness, moonrise, everything
    That is so silent, sweet, and pale:
    Come, so ye wake the nightingale.
       CHRISTINA GEORGINA ROSSETTI, *Bird Raptures*

Merrily swinging on brier and weed,
    Near to the nest of his little dame,
Over the mountain-side or mead,
    Robert of Lincoln is telling his name:
      Bob-o'-link, bob-o'-link,
      Spink, spank, spink;
Snug and safe is this nest of ours,
Hidden among the summer flowers.
      Chee, chee, chee.
      WILLIAM CULLEN BRYANT, *Robert of Lincoln*

June's bridesman, poet o' the year,
Gladness on wings, the bobolink, is here;
Half-hid in tip-top apple-blooms he swings,
Or climbs against the breeze with quiverin' wings,
Or, givin' way to 't in a mock despair,
Runs down, a brook o' laughter, thru the air.
JAMES RUSSELL LOWELL, *Biglow Papers*

Musical accompaniment to spring is provided by the silvery-voiced song sparrow.
ROGER TORY PETERSON, *Birds over America*

See how that pair of billing doves
With open murmurs own their loves
And, heedless of censorious eyes,
Pursue their unpolluted joys:
No fears of future want molest
The downy quiet of their nest.
MARY WORTLEY MONTAGU, *Verses Written in a Garden*

Bird of the broad and sweeping wing,
Thy home is high in heaven,
Where wide the storms their banners fling,
And the tempest clouds are driven.
JAMES GATES PERCIVAL, *To the Eagle*

When thou seest an eagle, thou seest a portion of Genius; lift up they head!
WILLIAM BLAKE, *Proverbs of Hell*

Flowers

A morning-glory at my window satisfies me more than the metaphysics of books.
WALT WHITMAN, *Song of Myself*

Not a flower
But shows some touch, in freckle, streak or stain,
Of His unrivall'd pencil.
WILLIAM COWPER, *The Task*

And because the breath of flowers is far sweeter in the air (where it comes and goes, like the warbling of music) than in the hand, therefore nothing is more fit for that delight than to know what be the flowers and plants that do best perfume the air.

FRANCIS BACON, Essays: Of Gardens

Thou blossom bright with autumn dew,
And colored with the heaven's own blue,
That openest when the quiet light
Succeeds the keen and frosty night.

WILLIAM CULLEN BRYANT, To the Fringed Gentian

Don't despise a flower because it is common.

ALFRED STEFFERUD, How to Know the Wild Flowers

Teach me the secret of thy loveliness,
That, being made wise, I may aspire to be
As beautiful in thought, and so express
Immortal truths to earth's mortality.

MADISON CAWEIN, To a Wind-Flower

They speak of hope to the fainting heart,
With a voice of promise they come and part,
They sleep in dust through the wintry hours,
They break forth in glory—bring flowers, bright flowers!

FELICIA DOROTHEA HEMANS, Bring Flowers

You buy some flowers for your table;
You tend them tenderly as you're able;
You fetch them water from hither and thither—
What thanks do you get for it all? They wither.

SAMUEL HOFFENSTEIN, Poems in Praise of Practically Nothing

Our rocks are rough, but smiling there
Th' acacia waves her yellow hair,
Lonely and sweet, nor loved the less
For flow'ring in a wilderness.

THOMAS MOORE, Lalla Rookh

Look at this vigorous plant that lifts its head
    from the meadow,
See how its leaves are turned to the north,
    as true as the magnet;
This is the compass-flower, that the finger of God
    has planted
Here in the houseless wild, to direct the traveller's journey.
                    LONGFELLOW, *Evangeline*

Mountain gorses, ever-golden,
Cankered not the whole year long!
Do ye teach us to be strong,
Howsoever pricked and holden
Like your thorny blooms, and so
Trodden on by rain and snow,
Up the hillside of this life, as bleak as where ye grow?
           E. B. BROWNING, *Lessons from the Gorse*

Flowers have an expression of countenance as much as men or animals. Some seem to smile; some have a sad expression; some are pensive and diffident; others again are plain, honest and upright, like the broad-faced sunflower and the hollyhock.
           HENRY WARD BEECHER, *Star Papers*

What are the flowers of Scotland,
    All others that excel?
The lovely flowers of Scotland,
    All others that excel!
The thistle's purple bonnet,
    And bonny heather bell,
Oh, they're the flowers of Scotland
    All others that excel!
          JAMES HOGG, *The Flowers of Scotland*

Sharing the stillness of the unimpassioned rock, they share also its endurance; and while the winds of departing Spring scatter the white hawthorn blossom like drifted snow, and summer dims on the parched meadow the drooping of its cowslip-gold, far above, among the mountains, the silver lichen-spots rest, starlike, on the stone; and the gathering orange stain upon the edge of yonder Western peak reflects the sunsets of a thousand years.
          JOHN RUSKIN, *Modern Painters*

Yet mark'd I where the bolt of Cupid fell:
It fell upon a little western flower,
Before milk-white, now purple with love's wound,
And maidens call it love-in-idleness.
Fetch me that flower; the herb I shew'd thee once:
The juice of it on sleeping eyelids laid
Will make or man or woman madly dote
Upon the next live creature that it sees.

     SHAKESPEARE, *A Midsummer-Night's Dream*

Lone Flower, hemmed in with snows and white as they
But hardier far, once more I see thee bend
Thy forehead, as if fearful to offend,
Like an unbidden guest. Though day by day,
Storms, sallying from the mountain tops, waylay
The rising sun, and on the plains descend;
Yet art thou welcome, welcome as a friend
Whose zeal outruns his promise!

     WORDSWORTH, *To a Snowdrop*

  Not one of Flora's brilliant race
    A form more perfect can display;
  Art could not feign more simple grace
    Nor Nature take a line away.
  JAMES MONTGOMERY, *On Planting a Tulip-Root*

If thou hast a loaf of bread, sell half and buy the flowers of
the narcissus; for bread nourisheth the body, but the narcissus
the soul.

     MOHAMMED

  And the Naiad-like lily of the vale,
  Whom youth makes so fair and passion so pale,
  That the light of its tremulous bells is seen,
  Through their pavilions of tender green.
    SHELLEY, *The Sensitive Plant*

  Heart's ease or pansy, pleasure or thought,
  Which would the picture give us of these?
  Surely the heart that conceived it sought
    Heart's ease.
    SWINBURNE, *A Flower Piece by Fantin*

The rose is fairest when 't is budding new,
    And hope is brightest when it dawns from fears;
The rose is sweetest washed with morning dew,
    And love is loveliest when embalmed in tears.
                SCOTT, *The Lady of the Lake*

    And the rose herself has got
    Perfume which on earth is not.
        KEATS, *Bards of Passion and of Mirth*

    Love dropp'd eyelids and a kiss,—
    Such our breath and blueness is.
          LEIGH HUNT, *Violets*

Oh, raise your deep-fringed lids that close
    To wrap you in some sweet dream's thrall;
I am the spectre of the rose
    You wore but last night at the ball.
    THÉOPHILE GAUTIER, *The Spectre of the Rose*

In that dark land of mystic dream
    Where dark Osiris sprung,
It bloomed beside his sacred stream
    While yet the world was young;
And every secret Nature told
    Of golden wisdom's power,
Is nestled still in every fold,
    Within the Lotos flower.
        WILLIAM WINTER, *A Lotos Flower*

    Light-enchanted Sunflower, thou
    Who gazest ever true and tender
    On the sun's revolving splendour!
        CALDERON, *El Mágico Prodigioso*

Farming and Country Living

I know few things more pleasing to the eye, or more capable
of affording scope and gratification to a taste for the beautiful,
than a well-situated, well-cultivated farm.
                      EDWARD EVERETT

He that by the Plough would thrive,
Himself must either hold or drive.
BENJAMIN FRANKLIN, *Poor Richard's Almanac*

One of the pleasant things about living in the country is that there aren't any holidays. One day is like the next and if you want a day off you can take it when you like. It doesn't have to be on the same day ninety million other people are having a holiday.

LOUIS BROMFIELD, *Malabar Farm*

Far back in the ages,
    The plough with wreaths was crowned;
The hands of kings and sages
    Entwined the chaplet round.
BRYANT, *Ode for an Agricultural Celebration*

To plow is to pray—to plant is to prophesy, and the harvest answers and fulfills.
R. G. INGERSOLL, *About Farming in Illinois*

O peasant, thou tillest the fields and fertilizest them, and sowest them. Thou makest the wheat to rise from the earth; through thee the "barren" is converted into grain; thou nourishest man, who is flesh. It is thanks to thy effort that we live here below. Glory to thee, O peasant.
JOSEPH ROUX, *Meditations of a Parish Priest*

Through the ample open door of the peaceful country barn,
A sun-lit pasture field, with cattle and horses feeding;
And haze, and vista, and the far horizon, fading away.
WALT WHITMAN, *A Farm Picture*

And he gave it for his opinion that whoever could make two ears of corn, or two blades of grass, to grow upon a spot of ground where only one grew before, would deserve better of mankind, and do more essential service to his country, than the whole race of politicians put together.
SWIFT, *Gulliver's Travels*

The life of the husbandman,—a life fed by the bounty of earth and sweetened by the airs of heaven.
DOUGLAS JERROLD, *The Husbandman's Life*

The glory of the farmer is that, in the division of labors, it is his part to create. All trade rests at last on his primitive activity.

EMERSON, *Society and Solitude*

There is nothing grateful but the earth; you cannot do too much for it: it will continue to repay tenfold the pains and labour bestowed upon it.

LORD RAVENSWORTH

'Tis sweet to spend one's time in the cultivation of the fields.

OVID, *Epistulae ex Ponto*

He (the husbandman) equalled the riches of kings in the happiness of his mind; and returning home in the late evening, loaded his board with feasts unbought.

VERGIL, *Georgics*

Heap high the farmer's wintry hoard!
Heap high the golden corn!
No richer gift has Autumn poured
From out her lavish horn!

WHITTIER, *The Corn-Song*

Far from the madding crowd's ignoble strife,
Their sober wishes never learn'd to stray;
Along the cool, sequester'd vale of life
They kept the noiseless tenor of their way.

THOMAS GRAY, *Elegy Written in a Country
Churchyard*

To one who has been long in city pent,
'Tis very sweet to look into the fair
And open face of heaven,—to breathe a prayer
Full in the smile of the blue firmament.

KEATS, *Sonnet*

A Look at the Heavens

The heavens declare the glory of God, and the firmament sheweth his handywork.

Old Testament: Psalms, XIX, 1

And they were canopied by the blue sky,
So cloudless, clear, and purely beautiful
That God alone was to be seen in heaven.
BYRON, *The Dream*

Bright star! would I were steadfast as thou art.
JOHN KEATS, *Sonnet*

Heaven's ebon vault,
Studded with stars unutterably bright,
Through which the moon's unclouded grandeur rolls,
Seems like a canopy which Love has spread
To curtain her sleeping world.
SHELLEY, *Queen Mab*

The spacious firmament on high,
With all the blue ethereal sky,
And spangled heavens, a shining frame,
Their great Original proclaim.
JOSEPH ADDISON

Over all the sky—the sky! far, far out of reach,
studded, breaking out, the eternal stars.
WALT WHITMAN, *Bivouac on a Mountain Side*

Wide are the meadows of night
And daisies are shining there,
Tossing their lovely dews,
Lustrous and fair;
And through these sweet fields go,
Wanderers amid the stars—
Venus, Mercury, Uranus, Neptune,
Saturn, Jupiter, Mars.
WALTER DE LA MARE, *Wanderers*

When he (the astronomer) peers through his telescope he
looks not only outward in space but backward in time. His
sensitive cameras can detect the glimmer of island universes
500 million light years away—faint gleams that began their
journey at a period of terrestrial time when the first vertebrates
were starting to crawl from warm Paleozoic seas onto the

young continents of Earth. His spectroscope tells him, moreover, that these huge outer systems are hurtling into limbo, away from our own galaxy, at incredible velocities ranging up to 35,000 miles a second.

LINCOLN BARNETT, *The Universe and Dr. Einstein*

There is one glory of the sun, and another glory of the moon, and another glory of the stars; for one star differeth from another star in glory.

New Testament: I Corinthians, xv, 41

Ye stars! which are the poetry of Heaven!
If in your bright leaves we would read the fate
Of man and empires,—'tis to be forgiven,
That in our aspirations to be great,
Our destinies o'erleap their mortal state,
And claim a kindred with you; for ye are
A beauty and a mystery, and create
In us such love and reverence from afar,
That fortune, fame, power, life, have
            named themselves a star.

BYRON, *Childe Harold*

Go and catch a falling star.

JOHN DONNE, *Song*

The stellar universe is still very young. It will take about 10 billion years more for our Sun completely to burn up its fuel and come to the end of its hydrogen evolution. On the other hand, there are definite indications that the whole stellar universe was formed not more than two billion years ago.

GEORGE GAMOW, *The Birth and Death of the Sun*

                The glorious sun,
Stays in his course and plays the alchemist,
Turning with splendour of his precious eye
The meagre cloddy earth to glittering gold.

SHAKESPEARE, *King John*

Now from the smooth deep ocean-stream the sun
Began to climb the heavens, and with new rays
Smote the surrounding fields.

HOMER, *Iliad* (Bryant transl.)

A late lark twitters from the quiet skies;
And from the west,
Where the sun, his day's work ended,
Lingers as in content,
There falls on the old, grey city
An influence luminous and serene,
A shining peace.

W. E. HENLEY, *Margaritae Sorori*

And God made two great lights, great for their use
To man, the greater to have rule by day,
The less by night altern.

MILTON, *Paradise Lost*

The stars draw back their shining faces when they surround
the fair moon in her silver fulness.

SAPPHO

The Mighty Sea

The sea lies all about us. The commerce of all lands must cross
it. The very winds that move over the lands have been cradled
on its broad expanse and seek ever to return to it. The continents themselves dissolve and pass to the sea, in grain after
grain of eroded land . . . In its mysterious past it encom-
passes all the dim origins of life and receives in the end, after,
it may be, many transmutations, the dead husks of that same
life. For all at last returns to the sea—the beginning and the
end.

RACHEL CARSON, *The Sea Around Us*

The sea hath no King but God alone.
DANTE GABRIEL ROSSETTI, *The White Ship*

The sea doth wash away all human ills.
EURIPIDES, *Iphigenia in Tauris*

Behold the Sea,
The opaline, the plentiful and strong,
Yet beautiful as is the rose in June,

Fresh as the trickling rainbow of July;
Sea full of food, the nourisher of kinds,
Purger of earth, and medicine of men;
Creating a sweet climate by my breath,
Washing out harms and griefs from memory,
And, in my mathematic ebb and flow,
Giving a hint of that which changes not.

EMERSON, *Sea-Shore*

The sea is like a splintered mirror.

ANTOINE DE SAINT EXUPÉRY, *Wind, Sand and Stars*

Sweet is the bitter sea, and the clear green in which the gaze seeks the soul, looking through the glass into itself. The sea thinks for me as I listen and ponder; the sea thinks, and every boom of the wave repeats my prayer.

RICHARD JEFFERIES, *The Story of My Heart*

Round the world and home again,
That's the sailor's way.

WILLIAM ALLINGHAM, *Homeward Bound*

They that go down to the sea in ships, that do business in great waters; these see the works of the Lord, and his wonders in the deep.

Old Testament: Psalms, CVII, 23, 24

Rivers and Brooks

A river is the cosiest of friends. You must love it and live with it before you can know it.

G. W. CURTIS, *Lotus-Eating*

The river glideth at his own sweet will.

WORDSWORTH, *Sonnet Composed upon Westminster Bridge*

Of nothing comes nothing: springs rise not above
    Their source in the far-hidden heart of the mountains:
Whence then have descended the Wisdom and Love
    That in man leap to light in intelligent fountains?

J. T. TROWBRIDGE, *The Missing Leaf*

The current that with gentle murmur glides,
Thou know'st, being stopp'd, impatiently doth rage;
But when his fair course is not hindered,
He makes sweet music with the enamell'd stones,
Giving a gentle kiss to every sedge
He overtaketh in his pilgrimage.
                    SHAKESPEARE, *The Two Gentlemen of Verona*

Ayr, gurgling, kiss'd his pebbled shore,
        O'erhung with wild woods thickening green;
    The fragrant birch and hawthorn hoar
        Twin'd amorous round the raptur'd scene.
                            BURNS, *Thou Lingering Star*

Then I saw the Congo, creeping through the black,
Cutting through the jungle with a golden track.
                        VACHEL LINDSAY, *The Congo*

And Potomac flowed calmly, scarce heaving her breast,
With her low-lying billows all bright in the west,
For a charm as from God lulled the waters to rest
        Of the fair-rolling river.
                PAUL HAMILTON HAYNE, *Beyond the Potomac*

            I chatter, chatter, as I flow
                To join the brimming river,
            For men may come and men may go,
                But I go on for ever.
                            TENNYSON, *The Brook*

            A noise like of a hidden brook
                In the leafy month of June,
            That to the sleeping woods all night
                Singeth a quiet tune.
                        COLERIDGE, *Ancient Mariner*

Shallow brooks murmur most, deep silent slide away.
                    SIR PHILIP SIDNEY, *Arcadia*

HISTORY

History and Historians

History, by apprising [men] of the past, will enable them to judge of the future.

THOMAS JEFFERSON, *Writings*

History, as it lies at the root of all science, is also the first distinct product of man's spiritual nature; his earliest expression of what can be called Thought.

THOMAS CARLYLE, *Essays: On History*

History should be guided by strict truth, and worthy actions require nothing more.

PLINY THE YOUNGER, *Epistles*

By this time, like one who had set out on his way by night, and travelled through a region of smooth or idle dreams, our history now arrives on the confines, where daylight and truth meet us with a clear dawn, representing to our view, though at a far distance, true colours and shapes.

JOHN MILTON, *History of Britain*

It is the true office of history to represent the events themselves, together with the counsels, and to leave the observations and conclusions thereupon to the liberty and faculty of every man's judgment.

FRANCIS BACON, *The Advancement of Learning*

Historians ought to be precise, faithful, and unprejudiced; and neither interest nor fear, hatred nor affection, should make them swerve from the way of truth.

CERVANTES, *Don Quixote*

To be a really good historian is perhaps the rarest of intellectual distinctions.

THOMAS BABINGTON MACAULAY, *Essays: History*

A teacher must either treat history as a catalogue, a record, a romance, or as an evolution.

HENRY ADAMS, *The Education of Henry Adams*

Peace on Earth

Peace is the healing and elevating influence of the world.
WOODROW WILSON, (from an Address in Philadelphia,
10 May, 1915)

Where there is peace, God is.
GEORGE HERBERT, *Jacula Prudentum*

How beautiful upon the mountains are feet of him that bringeth good tidings, that publisheth peace.
Old Testament: Isaiah, LII, 7

Glory to God in the highest, and on earth peace, good will toward men.
New Testament: Luke II, 14

Who gives a nation peace, gives tranquility to all.
HORACE WALPOLE, *Letter to Sir Horace Mann*

The curse of a universal state is that it is the result of a successful knock-out blow delivered by one sole surviving member of a group of contending military Powers. It is a product of that 'salvation by the sword' which we have seen to be no salvation at all. What we are looking for is a free consent of free peoples to dwell together in unity, and to make, uncoerced, the far-reaching adjustments and concessions without which this ideal cannot be realized in practice.
ARNOLD J. TOYNBEE, *A Study of History*

Peace cannot be kept by force. It can only be achieved by understanding.
ALBERT EINSTEIN

A peace is of the nature of a conquest;
For then both parties nobly are subdued,
And neither party loser.
SHAKESPEARE, *II Henry IV*

For lo! the days are hastening on,
By prophet-bards foretold,
When with the ever-circling years,
Comes round the age of gold;

When Peace shall over all the earth
   Its ancient splendors fling
And the whole world send back the song
   Which now the angels sing.
     EDMUND HAMILTON SEARS, *The Angels' Song*

Ah! when shall all men's good
Be each man's rule, and universal Peace
Lie like a shaft of light across the land,
And like a lane of beams athwart the sea?
     TENNYSON, *The Golden Year*

A federation of all humanity, together with a sufficient measure of social justice to ensure health, education, and a rough equality of opportunity, would mean such a release and increase of human energy as to open a new phase in human history.

     H. G. WELLS, *The Outline of History*

People and Politics

The safety of the people shall be the highest law.
     CICERO, *De Legibus*

I shall on all subjects have a policy to recommend, but none to enforce against the will of the people.
     ULYSSES S. GRANT, *First Inaugural Address*

A people's voice is a mighty power.
     AESCHYLUS, *Agamemnon*

Why should there not be a patient confidence in the ultimate justice of the people? Is there any better or equal hope in the world?

     ABRAHAM LINCOLN, *First Inaugural Address*

The people will come to their own at last,—
God is not mocked forever.
     JOHN HAY, *The Sphinx of the Tuileries*

The people's right remains; let those who dare
Dispute their power, when they the judges are.
     JOHN DRYDEN, *Character of a Good Parson*

Politics I conceive to be nothing more than the science of the ordered progress of society along the lines of greatest usefulness and convenience to itself.

WOODROW WILSON

There is a certain satisfaction in coming down to the lowest ground of politics, for we get rid of cant and hypocrisy.

EMERSON, *Representative Men*

When shall the softer, saner politics,
Whereof we dream, have play in each proud land?

THOMAS HARDY, *Departure*

I always voted at my party's call,
And never thought of thinking for myself at all!
I thought so little, they rewarded me
By making me the ruler of the Queen's navee!

W. S. GILBERT, *Pinafore*

A party of order or stability and a party of progress or reform are both necessary elements of a healthy state of political life.

JOHN STUART MILL, *On Liberty*

What is a communist? One who has yearnings
For equal division of unequal earnings.

EBENEZER ELLIOT, *Epigram*

Now warn't thet a system wuth pains in presarvin',
Where the people found jints an' their frien's done the
carvin?

JAMES RUSSELL LOWELL, *Biglow Papers*

The conduct of a wise politician is ever suited to the present posture of affairs. Often by foregoing a part he saves the whole, and by yielding in a small matter secures a greater.

PLUTARCH, *Lives: Publicola and Solon*

No man who ever held the office of President would congratulate a friend on obtaining it. He will make one man ungrateful, and a hundred men his enemies, for every office he can bestow.

JOHN ADAMS

All power is a trust; that we are accountable for its exercise; that from the people and for the people all springs, and all must exist.

BENJAMIN DISRAELI, *Vivian Grey*

Good Government

Government is a trust, and the officers of the government are trustees; and both the trust and the trustees are created for the benefit of the people.

HENRY CLAY, *Speech*

A wise and frugal government, which shall restrain men from injuring one another, which shall leave them otherwise free to regulate their own pursuits of industry and improvement, and shall not take from the mouth of labor the bread it has earned—this is the sum of good government.

THOMAS JEFFERSON

What government is the best? That which teaches us to govern ourselves.

GOETHE, *Sprüche in Prosa*

The aggregate happiness of society, which is best promoted by the practice of a virtuous policy, is, or ought to be, the end of all government.

GEORGE WASHINGTON

Every form of government tends to perish by excess of its basic principle.

WILL DURANT

Our object in the construction of the state is the greatest happiness of the whole, and not that of any one class.

PLATO, *The Republic*

The four pillars of government: religion, justice, counsel, treasure.

BACON, *Essays: Of Seditions*

God has chosen little nations as the vessels by which He carries his choicest wines to the lips of humanity to rejoice their hearts, to exalt their vision, to strengthen their faith.
DAVID LLOYD GEORGE, *Speech*

The true greatness of nations is in those qualities which constitute the greatness of the individual.
CHARLES SUMNER, *Oration on the True Grandeur of Nations*

Statesmen and the State

A disposition to preserve, and an ability to improve, taken together, would be my standard of a statesman.
EDMUND BURKE, *Reflections on the Revolution in France*

The first and essential quality towards being a statesman is to have a public spirit.
RICHARD STEELE, *The Tatler*

Statesman, yet friend to truth; of soul sincere,
In action faithful, and in honor clear;
Who broke no promise, serv'd no private end,
Who gain'd no title, and who lost no friend.
ALEXANDER POPE, *On James Craggs*

And statesmen at her council met
Who knew the seasons when to take
Occasion by the hand, and make
The bounds of freedom wider yet.
TENNYSON, *To the Queen*

Not stones, nor timber, nor the art of building constitute a state; but wherever men are who know how to defend themselves, there is a city and a fortress.
ALCAEUS, *Ode*

The worth of a State in the long run is the worth of the individuals composing it.
JOHN STUART MILL, *On Liberty*

For as, of all the ways of life, but one—
    The path of duty—leads to happiness;
So in their duty States must find at length
Their welfare, and their safety, and their strength.

ROBERT SOUTHEY, *Carmen Nuptiale*

It is for the good of nations, and not for the emolument or aggrandizement of particular individuals, that government ought to be established, and that mankind are at the expense of supporting it. The defects of every government and constitution both as to principle and form, must, on a parity of reasoning, be as open to discussion as the defects of a law, and it is a duty which every man owes to society to point them out.

THOMAS PAINE, *The Rights of Man*

The three great ends which a statesman ought to propose to himself in the government of a nation are: (1) security to possessors; (2) facility to acquirers; and (3) hope to all.

SAMUEL TAYLOR COLERIDGE, *Table-Talk*

I say the mission of government, henceforth, in civilized lands, is not repression alone, and not authority alone, not even of law, nor by that favorite standard of the eminent writer, the rule of the best men, the born heroes and captains of the race (as if such ever, or one time out of a hundred, get into the big places, elective or dynastic)—but higher than the highest arbitrary rule, to train communities through all their grades, beginning with individuals and ending there again, to rule themselves.

WALT WHITMAN, *Democratic Vistas*

States are as the men are; they grow out of the characters of men.

PLATO, *The Republic*

The principles of a free constitution are irrecoverably lost, when the legislative power is nominated by the executive.

EDWARD GIBBON, *Decline and Fall of the Roman Empire*

Progress of Civilization

Laws and institutions must go hand in hand with the progress of the human mind. As that becomes more developed, more enlightened, as new discoveries are made, new truths disclosed, and manners and opinions change with the change of circumstances, institutions must advance also, and keep pace with the times.

THOMAS JEFFERSON

Thoughtful men, once escaped from the blinding influences of traditional prejudice, will find in the lowly stock whence man has sprung the best evidence of the splendor of his capacities; and will discern in his long progress through the past a reasonable ground of faith in his attainment of the future.

THOMAS HENRY HUXLEY, *Evidence as to Man's Place in Nature*

Great historical movements are never begun for the attainment of remote and imperfectly comprehended ends. They demand something concrete to work for; they need clearly defined, particular aims.

JEAN L. JAURÉS, *Études socialistes*

Man, made of the dust of the world, does not forget his origin; and all that is yet inanimate will one day speak and reason. Unpublished nature will have its whole secret told.

EMERSON, *Uses of Great Men*

No one is so savage that he cannot become civilized, if he will lend a patient ear to culture.

HORACE, *Epistles*

In overcoming prejudice, working together is even more effective than talking together.

RALPH W. SOCKMAN

The history of civilization is the history of the slow and painful enfranchisement of the human race.

ROBERT G. INGERSOLL, *The Declaration of Independence*

New times demand new measures and new men;
The world advances, and in time outgrows
The laws that in our fathers' day were best;
And, doubtless, after us, some purer scheme
Will be shaped out by wiser men than we.
JAMES RUSSELL LOWELL, *A Glance Behind the Curtain*

Men, my brothers, men the workers, ever reaping something
    new:
That which they have done but earnest of the things that
    they shall do.

TENNYSON, *Locksley Hall*

And step by step, since time began,
    I see the steady gain of man.
JOHN GREENLEAF WHITTIER, *The Chapel of the Hermits*

The greatest task before civilization at present is to make
machines what they ought to be, the slaves, instead of the
masters of men.
HAVELOCK ELLIS, *Little Essays of Love and Virtue*

We believe that civilization has been built up, under the pres-
sure of the struggle for existence, by sacrifice in gratification
of the primitive impulses, and that it is to a great extent
forever being re-created, as each individual, successively join-
ing the community, repeats the sacrifice of his instinctive
pleasures for the common good.
SIGMUND FREUD, *A General Introduction to Psychoanalysis*

The test of our progress is not whether we add more to the
abundance of those who have much; it is whether we provide
enough for those who have too little.
FRANKLIN D. ROOSEVELT, *from his second Inaugural
address, 1937*

Liberty and Justice

Where the Spirit of the Lord is, there is liberty.
New Testament: II Corinthians, III, 17

The God who gave us life, gave us liberty at the same time.
THOMAS JEFFERSON

God makes no man a slave, no doubter free;
Abiding faith alone wins liberty.
JAMES JEFFREY ROCHE, *Washington*

Liberty, when it begins to take root, is a plant of rapid growth.
GEORGE WASHINGTON, *Maxims of Washington*

To those the truth makes free,
Sacred as truth itself is awful liberty.
AUBREY DE VERE, *Liberty*

But little do or can the best of us:
That little is achieved through Liberty.
ROBERT BROWNING, *Why I Am a Liberal*

Liberty, like day,
Breaks on the soul, and by a flash from Heav'n
Fires all the faculties with glorious joy.
WILLIAM COWPER, *The Task*

God grants liberty only to those who love it, and are always
ready to guard and defend it.
DANIEL WEBSTER

I sing of arms and the man.
VERGIL, *Aeneid*

Eternal Spirit of the chainless Mind!
Brightest in dungeons, Liberty! thou art,
For there thy habitation is the heart—
The heart which love of thee alone can bind.
BYRON, *The Prisoner of Chillon*

Stand fast therefore in the liberty wherewith Christ hath made
us free, and be not entangled again with the yoke of bondage.
New Testament: Galatians, v, 1

Justice is one; it binds all human society, and is based on one
law, which is right reason applied to command and prohibi-
tion.
CICERO, *De Legibus*

Justice is truth in action.
> BENJAMIN DISRAELI

Justice is the firm and continuous desire to render to everyone that which is his due.
> JUSTINIAN, *Institutiones*

Justice has nothing to do with expediency. Justice has nothing to do with any temporary standard whatever. It is rooted and grounded in the fundamental instincts of humanity.
> WOODROW WILSON, *Speech*

Where justice reigns, 'tis freedom to obey.
> JAMES MONTGOMERY, *Greenland*

There is no virtue so truly great and godlike as justice.
> JOSEPH ADDISON, *The Guardian*

The path of the just is as the shining light, that shineth more and more unto the perfect day.
> *Old Testament: Proverbs*, IV, 18

Exact justice is commonly more merciful in the long run than pity, for it tends to foster in men those stronger qualities which make them good citizens.
> JAMES RUSSELL LOWELL, *Among My Books*

And earthly power doth then show likest God's
When mercy seasons justice.
> SHAKESPEARE, *The Merchant of Venice*

In Freedom's Path

Who, then, is free? The wise who can command his passions, who fears not want, nor death, nor chains, firmly resisting his appetites and despising the honors of the world, who relies wholly on himself, whose angular points of character have all been rounded off and polished.
> HORACE, *Satires*

Freedom of men under government is to have a standing rule to live by, common to every one of that society, and made by the legislative power vested in it; a liberty to follow my own will in all things, when the rule prescribes not, and not to be subject to the inconstant, uncertain, unknown, arbitrary will of another man.

JOHN LOCKE, *Treatises on Government*

Free countries are those in which the rights of man are respected, and the laws, in consequence, are just.

ROBESPIERRE

The cause of freedom is identified with the destinies of humanity, and in whatever part of the world it gains ground, by and by it will be a common gain to all those who desire it.

LOUIS KOSSUTH

In giving freedom to the slave we assure freedom to the free, —honorable alike in what we give and what we preserve.

ABRAHAM LINCOLN, Message to Congress, Dec. 1, 1862

The United States, knowing no distinction of her own citizens on account of religion or nativity, naturally believes in a civilization the world over which will secure the same universal views.

ULYSSES S. GRANT

Is freedom anything but the right to live as we wish? Nothing else.

EPICTETUS, *Discourses*

Men are freest when they are most unconscious of freedom.
D. H. LAWRENCE, *Studies in Classic American Literature*

Freedom is re-created year by year,
In hearts wide open on the Godward side.
JAMES RUSSELL LOWELL, *Freedom*

Depend upon it, the lovers of freedom will be free.

EDMUND BURKE

Only free peoples can hold their purpose and their honor steady to a common end, and prefer the interests of mankind to any narrow interest of their own.

WOODROW WILSON (from his Address to Congress, asking declaration of war, April 2, 1917)

Aye, call it holy ground,
    The soil where first they trod!
They have left unstained what there they found—
    Freedom to worship God!

FELICIA DOROTHEA HEMANS, *Landing of the Pilgrim Fathers*

To speak his thoughts is every freeman's right,
In peace and war, in council and in fight.

HOMER, *Iliad* (Pope transl.)

In future days, which we seek to make secure, we look forward to a world founded upon four essential human freedoms. The first is freedom of speech and expression—everywhere in the world. The second is freedom of every person to worship God in his own way—everywhere in the world. The third is freedom from want—which, translated into world terms, means economic understandings which will secure to every nation a healthy peacetime life for its inhabitants—everywhere in the world. The fourth is freedom from fear—which, translated into world terms, means a world-wide reduction of armaments to such a point and in such a thorough fashion that no nation will be in a position to commit an act of physical aggression against any neighbor—anywhere in the world. That is no vision of a distant millennium. It is a definite basis for a kind of world attainable in our own time and generation.

FRANKLIN D. ROOSEVELT (Jan. 6, 1941)

Thoughts on Man

I believe that man will not merely endure: he will prevail. He is immortal, not because he alone among creatures has an inexhaustible voice but because he has a soul, a spirit capable of compassion and sacrifice and endurance. The poet's, the writer's, duty is to write about these things. It is his privilege to help man endure by lifting his heart, by reminding him of the courage and honor and hope and pride and compassion and pity and sacrifice which have been the glory of his past.

WILLIAM FAULKNER, in accepting the Nobel Prize in Literature at Stockholm, Sweden.

A man is the whole encyclopedia of facts. The creation of a thousand forests is in one acorn, and Egypt, Greece, Rome, Gaul, Britain, America, lie folded already in the first man.

EMERSON, *Essays*

No one expects Utopia, no one person can prepare a land fit for heroes, but almost any one can try to understand the past and the present in order to enrich the future.

HOUSTON PETERSON

Man is but a reed, the weakest in nature, but he is a thinking reed.

PASCAL, *Pensées*

Freedom of judgment can be attained only when we learn to estimate an individual according to his own ability and character. Then we shall find, if we were to select the best of mankind, that all races and all nationalities would be represented. Then we shall treasure and cultivate the variety of forms that human thought and activity has taken, and abhor, as leading to complete stagnation, all attempts to impress one pattern of thought upon whole nations or even upon the whole world.

FRANZ BOAS, *The Mind of Primitive Man*

In human works, tho' labour'd on with pain,
A thousand movements scarce one purpose gain;
In God's, one single can its end produce,
Yet serve to second too some other use:
So man, who here seems principal alone,
Perhaps acts second to some sphere unknown,
Touches some wheel, or verges to some goal:
'Tis but a part we see, and not a whole.

POPE, *Essay on Man*

It is easier to know mankind in general than man individually.
LA ROCHEFOUCAULD, *Maximes*

There is a book into which some of us are happily led to look, and to look again, and never tire of looking. It is the Book of Man. You may open that book whenever and wherever you find another human voice to answer yours, and another human hand to take in your own.
WALTER BESANT, *Books Which Have Influenced Me*

Man and his littleness perish, erased like an error and
cancelled;
Man and his greatness survive, lost in the greatness of God.
WILLIAM WATSON, *Hymn to the Sea*

There wanted yet the master work, the end
Of all yet done; a creature who not prone
And brute as other creatures, but endued
With sanctity of reason, might erect
His stature, and upright with front serene
Govern the rest, self-knowing, and from thence
Magnanimous to correspond with Heav'n.
MILTON, *Paradise Lost*

The true science and study of man is man.
PIERRE CHARRON

Say, why was man so eminently raised
Amid the vast creation? why ordained
Through life and death to dart his piercing eye,
With thoughts beyond the limit of his frame?
MARK AKENSIDE, *The Pleasures of Imagination*

In the whole history of mankind, far back into the dim past before man knew how to record thoughts or events, the human race has been distinguished from other forms of life by the existence—the fact—of religion. Periodic ..ttempts to deny God have always come and will always come to naught.
FRANKLIN DELANO ROOSEVELT

RELAXATION

Sweetly Doing Nothing

You should do nothing that did not absolutely *please* you.
Be idle, be very idle! The habits of your mind are such that
you will necessarily do much; but be as idle as you can.
SAMUEL TAYLOR COLERIDGE, *Letter to Southey*

It is impossible to enjoy idling thoroughly unless one has
plenty of work to do.
JEROME K. JEROME, *Idle Thoughts of an Idle Fellow*

We would all be idle if we could.
SAMUEL JOHNSON, (Boswell's *Life*)

There is one piece of advice, in a life of study, which I think
no one will object to; and that is, every now and then to be
completely idle,—to do nothing at all.
SYDNEY SMITH, *Sketches of Moral Philosophy*

Life does not agree with philosophy: there is no happiness
without idleness, and only the useless is pleasurable.
CHEKHOV, *Note-Books*

I loafe and invite my soul,
I lean and loafe at my ease observing a spear of summer grass.
WALT WHITMAN, *Song of Myself*

When a man's busy, why, leisure
Strikes him as wonderful pleasure;
'Faith, and at leisure once is he?
Straightway he wants to be busy.
ROBERT BROWNING, *The Glove*

What is more delightful than lettered ease?
CICERO, *Tusculanarum Disputationum*

A poor life this if, full of care,
We have no time to stand and stare.
WILLIAM H. DAVIES, *Leisure*

Give time to your friends, leisure to your wife, relax your mind, give rest to your body, so that you may the better fulfil your accustomed occupation.

PHAEDRUS, *Fables*

The wisdom of a learned man cometh by opportunity of leisure.

Apocrypha: Ecclesiasticus XXXVIII, 24

Pursuit of Pleasure

Then top and maintop crowd the sail,
    Heave Care owre side!
And large, before Enjoyment's gale,
    Let's tak' the tide.

ROBERT BURNS, *Epistle to James Smith*

It is impossible to live pleasantly without living wisely and well and justly; and it is impossible to live wisely and well and justly without living pleasantly.

EPICURUS, *Sovran Maxims*

There are only three pleasures in life pure and lasting, and all are derived from inanimate things—books, pictures, and the face of nature.

WILLIAM HAZLITT, *Criticisms on Art*

In life there is nothing more unexpected and surprising than the arrivals and departures of pleasure. If we find it in one place to-day, it is vain to seek it there to-morrow. You can not lay a trap for it.

ALEXANDER SMITH, *City Poem: A Boy's Dream*

Who will in time present from pleasure refrain,
Shall in time to come the more pleasure obtain.

JOHN HEYWOOD, *Proverbs*

His own special pleasure attracts each one.

VERGIL, *Eclogues*

Pleasure in moderation relaxes and tempers the spirit.

SENECA, *De Ira*

The shortest pleasures are the sweetest.
                              FARQUHAR, *The Twin Rivals*

Pleasure is necessarily reciprocal; no one feels, who does not
at the same time give it. To be pleased one must please.
                              LORD CHESTERFIELD, *Letters*

Holidays

If all the year was playing holidays,
To sport would be as tedious as to work.
                              SHAKESPEARE, *I Henry IV*

Time for work,—yet take
Much holiday for art's and friendship's sake.
GEORGE JAMES DE WILDE, *On the Arrival of Spring*

Come, bring with a noise,
My merry, merry boys,
The Christmas log to the firing;
While my good dame, she
Bids ye all be free;
And drink to your hearts' desiring.
          ROBERT HERRICK, *Ceremonies for Christmas*

Of all the days that's in the week
    I dearly love but one day—
And that's the day that comes betwixt
    A Saturday and Monday;
For then I'm drest all in my best
    To walk abroad with Sally;
She is the darling of my heart,
    And she lives in our alley.
          HENRY CAREY, *Sally in Our Alley*

The holiest of all holidays are those
    Kept by ourselves in silence and apart;
    The secret anniversaries of the heart,
When the full river of feeling overflows;—
The happy days unclouded to their close;

The sudden joys that out of darkness start
As flames from ashes; swift desires that dart
Like swallows singing down each wind that blows!
　　　　　　　　　　　　LONGFELLOW, *Holidays*

'Tis sweet to him, who all the week
　　Through city-crowds must push his way,
To stroll alone through fields and woods,
　　And hallow thus the Sabbath-day.
　　　　　　SAMUEL TAYLOR COLERIDGE, *Home-Sick*

To be able to fill leisure intelligently is the last product of
civilization.
　　　　　　BERTRAND RUSSELL, *Conquest of Happiness*

Horse and Hunt

The horn of the hunter is heard on the hill.
　　　　　　JULIA CRAWFORD, *Kathleen Mavourneen*

The dusky night rides down the sky,
　　And ushers in the morn;
The hounds all join in glorious cry,
　　The huntsman winds his horn;
　　　　And a-hunting we will go.
　　　　HENRY FIELDING, *Don Quixote in England*

Soon as Aurora drives away the night,
And edges eastern clouds with rosy light,
The healthy huntsman, with the cheerful horn,
Summons the dogs, and greets the dappled Morn.
　　　　　　　　　　JOHN GAY, *Rural Sports*

Hunting I reckon very good
To brace the nerves, and stir the blood:
Hygeia's sons with hound and horn,
And jovial cry awake the Morn.
　　　　　　　　MATTHEW GREEN, *The Spleen*

The horn, the horn, the lusty horn
Is not a thing to laugh to scorn.
　　　　　　SHAKESPEARE, *As You Like It*

D'ye ken John Peel with his coat so gay?
D'ye ken John Peel at the break of day?
D'ye ken John Peel when he's far, far away,
With his hounds and his horn in the morning?

> ANONYMOUS, *John Peel*

The woods are made for the hunters of dreams,
 The brooks for the fishers of song;
To the hunters who hunt for the gunless game
 The streams and the woods belong.

> SAM WALTER FOSS, *Bloodless Sportsmen*

Of horn and morn, and hark and bark,
 And echo's answering sounds,
All poets' wit hath ever writ
 In dog-rel verse of hounds.

> THOMAS HOOD, *The Epping Hunt*

A canter is the cure for every evil.

> BENJAMIN DISRAELI, *The Young Duke*

I saw young Harry, with his beaver on,
His cuisses on his thighs, gallantly arm'd
Rise from the ground like feather'd Mercury,
And vaulted with such ease into his seat
As if an angel dropp'd down from the clouds,
To turn and wind a fiery Pegasus
And witch the world with noble horsemanship.

> SHAKESPEARE, *I Henry IV*

The seat on a horse makes gentlemen of some and grooms of others.

> CERVANTES, *Don Quixote*

Good horses make short miles.

> GEORGE HERBERT, *Jacula Prudentum*

The Squire will wind up with an apocryphal saying—'there's nothing so good for the inside of a man as the outside of a horse.'

> G. W. E. RUSSELL, *Social Silhouettes*

Gamarra is a dainty steed,
Strong, black, and of a noble breed,
Full of fire, and full of bone,
With all his line of fathers known;
Fine his nose, his nostrils thin,
But blown abroad by the pride within!
His mane is like a river flowing,
And his eyes like embers glowing
In the darkness of the night,
And his pace as swift as light.

> BRYAN WALLER PROCTER, *The Blood Horse*

The valiant horse races best, at the barrier's fall, when he has others to follow and o'erpass.

> OVID, *The Art of Love*

Anglers' Delights

They say fish should swim thrice: first it should swim in the sea, then it should swim in the butter, and at last, sirrah, it should swim in good claret.

> JONATHAN SWIFT, *Polite Conversation*

Oh, you who've been a-fishing will endorse me when I say
That it always *is* the biggest fish you catch that gets away.

> EUGENE FIELD, *Our Biggest Fish*

You must lose a fly to catch a trout.

> GEORGE HERBERT, *Jacula Prudentum*

Our plenteous streams a various race supply,
The bright-eyed perch with fins of Tyrian dye,
The silver eel, in shining volumes, roll'd,
The yellow carp, in scales bedropp'd with gold,
Swift trouts, diversified with crimson stains,
And pikes, the tyrants of the wat'ry plains.

> ALEXANDER POPE, *Windsor Forest*

Inch for inch and pound for pound, the gamest fish that swims.

> JAMES A. HENSHALL, *Book of the Black Bass*

Still he fishes that catches one.

> THOMAS FULLER, *Gnomologia*

The first men that our Saviour dear
Did choose to wait upon Him here,
Blest fishers were; and fish the last
Food was, that He on earth did taste:
I therefore strive to follow those,
Whom He to follow Him hath chose.

IZAAK WALTON, *The Complete Angler: The Angler's Song*

Then come, my friend, forget your foes, and leave
  your fears behind,
And wander forth to try your luck, with cheerful, quiet mind.

HENRY VAN DYKE, *The Angler's Reveille*

Of all the world's enjoyments
  That ever valued were,
There's none of our employments
  With fishing can compare.

THOMAS D'URFEY, *Pills to Purge Melancholy*

Pleasures of Reading

Read, mark, learn, and inwardly digest.

Book of Common Prayer

There is an art of reading, as well as an art of thinking, and
an art of writing.

ISAAC D'ISRAELI, *Literary Character*

All good and true book-lovers practise the pleasing and im-
proving avocation of reading in bed.

EUGENE FIELD, *Love Affairs of a Bibliomaniac*

We get no good
By being ungenerous, even to a book,
And calculating profits,—so much help
By so much reading. It is rather when
We gloriously forget ourselves and plunge
Soul-forward, headlong, into a book's profound,
Impassioned for its beauty and salt of truth—
'Tis then we get the right good from a book.

E. B. BROWNING, *Aurora Leigh*

The mind, relaxing into needful sport,
Should turn to writers of an abler sort,
Whose wit well manag'd, and whose classic style,
Give truth a lustre, and make wisdom smile.

WILLIAM COWPER, *Retirement*

No man can read with profit that which he cannot learn to read with pleasure.

NOAH PORTER, *Books and Reading*

Reading is to the mind, what exercise is to the body. As by the one, health is preserved, strengthened, and invigorated; by the other, virtue, which is the health of the mind, is kept alive, cherished, and confirmed.

JOSEPH ADDISON, *The Tatler*

Let us assume that entertainment is the sole end of reading; even so, I think you would hold that no mental employment is so broadening to the sympathies or so enlightening to the understanding. Other pursuits belong not to all times, all ages, all conditions; but this gives stimulus to our youth and diversion to our old age; this adds a charm to success, and offers a haven of consolation to failure. Through the night-watches, on all our journeyings, and in our hours of ease, it is our unfailing companion.

CICERO, *Pro Archia Poeta*

It is a tie between men to have read the same book.

EMERSON, *Journals*

I was so allured to read that no recreation came to me better welcome.

MILTON, *An Apology for Smectymnuus*

To love to read is to exchange hours of ennui for hours of delight.

MONTESQUIEU, *Pensées*

The habit of reading is the only enjoyment in which there is no alloy; it lasts when all other pleasures fade.

ANTHONY TROLLOPE

Travel

For my part, I travel not to go anywhere, but to go. I travel for travel's sake. The great affair is to move.
ROBERT LOUIS STEVENSON, *Virginibus Puerisque: El Dorado*

A wise traveler never despises his own country.
GOLDONI, *Pamela*

He saw the cities of many men and knew their manners.
HOMER, *Odyssey*

For always roaming with a hungry heart,
Much have I seen and known,—cities of men
And manners, climates, councils, governments.
TENNYSON, *Ulysses*

As the Spanish proverb says, "He who would bring home the wealth of the Indies, must carry the wealth of the Indies with him." So it is in traveling; a man must carry knowledge with him, if he would bring home knowledge.
SAMUEL JOHNSON, (Boswell's *Life*)

Young men should travel, if but to amuse themselves.
BYRON, *Don Juan*

Voyage, travel and change of place impart vigour.
SENECA, *De Tranquillitate Animi*

He travels the fastest who travels alone.
RUDYARD KIPLING, *The Winners*

The soul of a journey is liberty, perfect liberty, to think, feel, do just as one pleases. We go a journey chiefly to be free of all impediments and of all inconveniences; to leave ourselves behind, much more to get rid of others.
WILLIAM HAZLITT, *On Going a Journey*

Afoot and light-hearted I take to the open road,
Healthy, free, the world before me,
The long brown path before me leading wherever I choose.
WALT WHITMAN, *Song of the Open Road*

Sleep and Rest

We sleep, but the loom of life never stops and the pattern
which was weaving when the sun went down is weaving when
it comes up to-morrow.

HENRY WARD BEECHER, *Life Thoughts*

Sleep, Silence' child, sweet father of soft rest,
Prince whose approach peace to all mortals brings,
Indifferent host to shepherds and to kings,
Sole comforter of minds with grief opprest.

WILLIAM DRUMMOND, *Sonnets*

O magic sleep! O comfortable bird,
That broodest o'er the troubled sea of the mind
Till it is hush'd and smooth!

KEATS, *Endymion*

O Sleep, thou rest of all things, Sleep, gentlest of the
Gods, peace of the soul, who puttest care to flight.

OVID, *Metamorphoses*

Sleep that knits up the ravell'd sleeve of care,
The death of each day's life, sore labour's bath,
Balm of hurt minds, great nature's second course,
Chief nourisher in life's feast.

SHAKESPEARE, *Macbeth*

Sleep after toil, port after stormy seas.

EDMUND SPENSER, *The Faerie Queene*

To all, to each, a fair good-night,
And pleasing dreams, and slumbers light!

SIR WALTER SCOTT, *Marmion*

I will both lay me down in peace, and sleep: for thou, Lord,
only makest me dwell in safety.

Old Testament: Psalms, IV, 8

Come unto me, all ye that labour and are heavy laden, and I
will give you rest.

New Testament: Matthew, XI, 28

Ah, what is more blessed than to put care aside, when the mind lays down its burden, and spent with distant travel, we come home again and rest on the couch we longed for? This, this alone, is worth all such toils.

CATULLUS, *Odes*

Joy as Relaxation

A good laugh is sunshine in a house.
THACKERAY, *Sketches: Love, Marriage*

The day most wholly lost is the one on which one does not laugh.
NICOLAS CHAMFORT, *Maximes et Pensées*

Laugh when I am merry, and claw no man in his humour.
SHAKESPEARE, *Much Ado About Nothing*

'Tis a good thing to laugh at any rate; and if a straw can tickle a man, it is an instrument of happiness.
JOHN DRYDEN, *Essays*

In laughter there is always a kind of joyousness that is incompatible with contempt or indignation.
VOLTAIRE, *L'Enfant Prodigue*

To-day, whatever may annoy,
The word for me is Joy, just simple Joy.
JOHN KENDRICK BANGS, *The Word*

It is a fine seasoning for joy to think of those we love.
MOLIÉRE, *Le Misanthrope*

O God, may I live to have one day of unsullied joy!
LUDWIG VAN BEETHOVEN

Oh, frabjous day! Callooh! Callay!
He chortled in his joy.
LEWIS CARROLL, *Through the Looking-Glass*

WITH A MERRY HEART

A Sense of Humor

True humor springs not more from the head than from the heart; it is not contempt, its essence is love; it issues not in laughter, but in still smiles, which lie far deeper. It is a sort of inverse sublimity, exalting, as it were, into our affections what is below us, while sublimity draws down into our affections what is above us.

THOMAS CARLYLE

Good sense is at the bottom of everything: virtue, genius, wit, talent and taste.

MARIE JOSEPH DE CHÉNIER

A sense of humour keen enough to show a man his own absurdities will keep him from the commission of all sins, or nearly all, save those that are worth committing.

SAMUEL BUTLER, *Life and Habit*

No mind is thoroughly well organized that is deficient in a sense of humour.

SAMUEL TAYLOR COLERIDGE, *Table Talk*

Humor's the true democracy.

ROBERT UNDERWOOD JOHNSON, *Divided Honors*

Everything is funny as long as it is happening to somebody else.

WILL ROGERS, *The Illiterate Digest*

Humour is odd, grotesque, and wild,
Only by affectation spoiled;
'Tis never by invention got;
Man have it when they know it not.

JONATHAN SWIFT, *To Mr. Delany*

A little nonsense now and then
Is relished by the wisest men.

ANONYMOUS

It is not in the power of every one to taste humor, however he may wish it; it is the gift of God! and a true feeler always brings half the entertainment along with him.

LAURENCE STERNE

For health and the constant enjoyment of life, give me a keen and ever present sense of humor; it is the next best thing to an abiding faith in providence.

GEORGE B. CHEEVER

The Point of Jest

Many a true word is spoken in jest.

English Proverb

He that laughs at his own jest mars all the mirth of it.

JAMES KELLY, Scottish Proverbs

Jesters do oft prove prophets.

SHAKESPEARE, King Lear

If a thing is spoken in jest, it is not fair to take it seriously.

PLAUTUS, Amphitruo

Jests that give pain are no jests.

CERVANTES, Don Quixote

Be not affronted at a jest; if one throw ever so much salt at thee thou wilt receive no harm unless thou art raw and ulcerous.

JUNIUS

Laughter should dimple the cheek, not furrow the brow. A jest should be such that all shall be able to join in the laugh which it occasions; but if it bears hard upon one of the company, like the crack of a string, it makes a stop in the music.

OWEN FELTHAM

Of all the griefs that harass the distress'd,
Sure the most bitter is a scornful jest.
Fate never wounds more deep the generous heart,
Than when a blockhead's insult points the dart.

SAMUEL JOHNSON

He who never relaxes into sportiveness is a wearisome companion; but beware of him who jests at everything! Such men disparage by some ludicrous association all objects which are presented to their thoughts, and thereby render themselves incapable of any emotion which can either elevate or soften them; they bring upon their moral being an influence more withering than the blasts of the desert.

ROBERT SOUTHEY

Laughter and Life

Laugh and be fat, sir.

BEN JONSON

A good laugh is sunshine in a house.

WILLIAM MAKEPEACE THACKERAY

Men show their character in nothing more clearly than by what they think laughable.

GOETHE

You hear that boy laughing?—you think he's all fun;
But the angels laugh, too, at the good he has done;
The children laugh loud as they troop to his call,
And the poor man that knows him laughs loudest of all.

OLIVER WENDELL HOLMES

If we consider the frequent reliefs we receive from laughter, and how often it breaks the gloom which is apt to depress the mind, one would take care not to grow too wise for so great a pleasure of life.

JOSEPH ADDISON

A laugh, to be joyous, must flow from a joyous heart, for without kindness there can be no true joy.

THOMAS CARLYLE

Without love and laughter there is no joy; live amid love and laughter.

HORACE, *Epistles*

Laugh and be well.

MATTHEW GREEN, *The Spleen*

When the green woods laugh with the voice of joy,
And the dimpling stream runs laughing by;
When the air does laugh with our merry wit,
And the green hill laughs with the noise of it.
                          WILLIAM BLAKE, *Laughing Song*

Very sound of very light,
Heard from morning's rosiest height,
When the soul of all delight,
    Fills a child's clear laughter.
              SWINBURNE, *A Child's Laughter*

One inch of joy surmounts of grief a span,
Because to laugh is proper to the man.
                                      RABELAIS

Laugh away, you fine laugher.
              MOLIÉRE, *L'École des Maris*

He laughs best that laughs last.
                        OLD PROVERB

Mirth and Merriment

An ounce of mirth is worth a pound of sorrow.
              RICHARD BAXTER, *Self-Denial*

Mirth's concussions rip the outward case,
And plant the stitches in a tenderer place.
    OLIVER WENDELL HOLMES, *A Rhymed Lesson*

Let your mirth be ever void of scurrility and biting words to
any man, for a wound given by a word is oftentimes harder
to be cured than that which is given with the sword.
    SIR HENRY SIDNEY, *Letter to His Son, Sir Philip Sidney*

The gift of gaiety may itself be the greatest good fortune, and
the most serious step toward maturity.
                                      IRWIN EDMAN

A merry heart maketh a cheerful countenance.
>   *Old Testament: Proverbs*, xv, 13

A man hath no better thing under the sun, than to eat, and to drink, and to be merry.
>   *Old Testament: Ecclesiastes*, VIII, 15

> In Paris a queer little man you may see,
>   A little man all in gray;
> Rosy and round as an apple is he,
> Content with the present whate'er it may be,
> While from care and from cash he is equally free,
>   And merry both night and day!
> "Ma foi! I laugh at the world," says he,
> "I laugh at the world, and the world laughs at me!"
>   What a gay little man in gray.
> PIERRE JEAN DE BÉRANGER, *The Little Man all in Gray*

>   Put on
> Your boldest suit of mirth, for we have friends
> That purpose merriment.
>   SHAKESPEARE, *The Merchant of Venice*

> Merry have we met, and merry have we been;
> Merry let us part, and merry meet again;
> With our merry sing-song, happy, gay, and free,
> With a merry ding-dong, happy let us be!
>   OLD ENGLISH RHYME

Epigrams

> What is an epigram? A dwarfish whole,
> Its body brevity, and wit its soul.
>   SAMUEL TAYLOR COLERIDGE

In general I don't see how an epigram, being a pure bolt from the blue, with no introduction or cue, gets itself writ.
>   WILLIAM JAMES, *Letters*

The qualities rare in a bee that we meet,
    In an epigram never should fail;
The body should always be little and sweet,
    And a sting should be felt in its tail.
              TOMAS DE YRIARTE, *The Epigram*

The Soul of Wit

Wit and wisdom are born with a man.
              JOHN SELDEN, *Table-Talk*

    Wit is the only wall
    Between us and the dark.
              MARK VAN DOREN, *Wit*

Generally speaking there is more wit than talent in this world.
Society swarms with witty people who lack talent.
              DE RIVAROL, *On Madame de Staël*

Look, he's winding up the watch of his wit; by and by it will
strike.
              SHAKESPEARE, *The Tempest*

Silence is the unbearable repartee.
              G. K. CHESTERTON

We have all of us sufficient fortitude to bear the misfortunes
of others.
              LA ROCHEFOUCAULD

The longer I live the more keenly I feel that whatever was
good enough for our fathers is not good enough for us.
              OSCAR WILDE

La Gabrielli, a celebrated singer, having asked 5,000 ducats
from the Empress of Russia as her fee for singing at St.
Petersburg for two months, the latter replied: "I pay none
of my field marshals on that scale." "In that case," said La
Gabrielli, "Your Majesty has only to make your field marshals
sing." The Empress paid the 5,000 ducats without further
demur.
              NICHOLAS CHAMFORT

A man's real life is that accorded to him in the thoughts of other men by reason of respect or natural love.

JOSEPH CONRAD

Divorce dates from just about the same time as marriage; I think that marriage is a few weeks the more ancient.

VOLTAIRE

A woman's preaching is like a dog's walking on his hind legs. It is not done well: but you are surprised to find it done at all.

SAMUEL JOHNSON

Woman is a delightful musical instrument, of which love is the bow, and man the artist.

STENDHAL

There are certain things which are intolerable when second-rate: poetry, music, painting, and public speaking.

JEAN DE LA BRUYÉRE

Do not be fooled into believing that because a man is rich he is necessarily smart. There is ample proof to the contrary.

JULIUS ROSENWALD

Brevity is the soul of wit.

SHAKESPEARE, *Hamlet*

Petty vexations may at times be petty, but still they are vex-ations. The smallest and most inconsiderable annoyances are the most piercing. As small letters weary the eyes most, so also the smallest affairs disturb us most.

MICHAEL DE MONTAIGNE

He who wishes to secure the good of others has already secured his own.

CONFUCIUS

When people complain of life, it is almost always because they have asked impossible things from it.

ERNEST RENAN

Advice is like kissing: it costs nothing, and it is a pleasant thing to do.

H. W. SHAW

Always advise a Friend to do that which you are sure he is not going to do. Then, if his Venture fails, you will receive credit for having warned him. If it succeeds, he will be happy in the Opportunity to tell you that you were Dead Wrong.

GEORGE ADE, *Fables in Slang*

We find ourselves less witty in remembering what we have said than in dreaming what we would have said.

J. PETIT-SENN

The last thing we decide when we write a book is what we shall put first.

BLAISE PASCAL, *Pensées*

Sallies and Fancies

Then read my fancies; they will stick like burrs.

JOHN BUNYAN, *The Pilgrim's Progress*

Fancy is a wilful imagination, a spontaneous act; fancy, a play as with dolls and puppets which we choose to call men and women; imagination, a perception and affirming of a real relation between a thought and some material fact. Fancy amuses; imagination expands and exalts us.

RALPH WALDO EMERSON, *Poetry and Imagination*

Everybody likes and respects self-made men. It is a great deal better to be made that way than not to be made at all.

OLIVER WENDELL HOLMES

Genius is one per cent inspiration and ninety-nine per cent perspiration.

THOMAS A. EDISON

Reputation is in itself only a farthing candle, of a wavering and uncertain flame, and easily blown out, but it is the light by which the world looks for and finds merit.

JAMES RUSSELL LOWELL

There are obviously two educations. One should teach us how to make a living, and the other how to live.

JAMES TRUSLOW ADAMS

The wise carry their knowledge as they do their watches, not for display, but for their own use.

SIR THOMAS BROWNE

When a true genius appears in the world, you may know him by this sign, that the dunces are all in confederacy against him.

JONATHAN SWIFT

The least pain in our little finger gives us more concern and uneasiness, than the destruction of millions of our fellow-beings.

WILLIAM HAZLITT

Whimsies and Witticisms

He was so benevolent, so merciful a man, that, in his mistaken compassion, he would have held an umbrella over a duck in a shower of rain.

JERROLD

Nothing between humans is one to three. In fact, I long ago come to the conclusion that all life is six to five against.

DAMON RUNYON

I gravely doubt whether women were ever married by capture. I think they pretended to be; as they do still.

G. K. CHESTERTON

When a woman has ceased to be quite the same to us, it matters little how different she becomes.

WALTER SAVAGE LANDOR

The distinction between a witticism and a low, rude joke is that the former may be indulged in, if it be seasonable, and in hours of relaxation, by a virtuous man; the latter is unworthy of any human being.

CICERO, *De Officiis*

When flatterers compliment kings for virtues that are the very reverse of their characters, they remind me of the story of a little boy who was apt to tell people of any remarkable defect in their persons. One day a gentleman who had an extraordinary large nose being to dine with the boy's parents, his mother charged him not to say anything of the gentleman's large nose. When he arrived, the child stared at him, and then, turning to his mother, said, "Mamma, what a pretty little nose that gentleman has!"

HORACE WALPOLE

Impromptu is truly the touchstone of wit.

MOLIÉRE, *Les Précieuses Ridicules*

Critics are men who have failed in literature and art.

BENJAMIN DISRAELI

A book should have no more than the requisite tincture of wit; but a superabundance is quite allowable in conversation.

JOSEPH JOUBERT

Odds and Ends

'Tis strange what a man may do, and a woman yet think him an angel.

WILLIAM MAKEPEACE THACKERAY

A bill is the most extraordinary locomotive engine that the genius of man ever produced. It would keep on running, during the longest lifetime, without ever once stopping of its own accord.

CHARLES DICKENS

The difference between a human being ten years of age and one fifty years of age lies altogether in the matter of toys.

AUSTIN O'MALLEY

From the point of view of morals, life seems to be divided into two periods; in the first we indulge, in the second we preach.

WILL DURANT

I might give my life for my friend, but he had better not ask me to do up a parcel.

LOGAN PEARSALL SMITH

Academies sometimes honour genius, but cannot cultivate or protect it.

HOLBROOK JACKSON

Man nor king can see unmoved the coming of a windfilled sail, the coming of a lovely lady, the coming of a horse in speed.

JAMES STEPHENS

Like women, sail ships have *skirts, aprons, hoops, bonnets, earrings, stays, caps,* even *husbands.*

ANONYMOUS

As man is now constituted, to be brief is almost a condition of being inspired.

GEORGE SANTAYANA

Methods of locomotion have improved greatly in recent years, but places to go remain about the same.

DON HEROLD

He who can, does; he who cannot, teaches.

GEORGE BERNARD SHAW

Man is the only animal that blushes. Or needs to.

MARK TWAIN

Be sparing of speech, and things will come right of themselves.

LAO-TSZE

THE WORLD'S WORK

Our Home, the Earth

There are two worlds; the world that we can measure with line and rule, and the world that we feel with our hearts and imagination.

LEIGH HUNT, *Men, Women and Books*

The whole Creation is a mystery and particularly that of man.

Sir THOMAS BROWNE, *Religio Medici*

What a dark world—who knows?—
Ours to inhabit is!
One touch and what a strange
Glory might burst on us,
What a hid universe!

ISRAEL ZANGWILL, *Blind Children*

The world belongs to those who think and act with it, who keep a finger on its pulse.

DEAN W. R. INGE

All the world's a stage.
And all the men and women merely players:
They have their exits and their entrances;
And one man in his time plays many parts.

SHAKESPEARE, *As You Like It*

O world, as God has made it! All is beauty:
And knowing this, is love, and love is duty.
What further may be sought for or declared?

ROBERT BROWNING, *The Guardian-Angel*

The world is so full of a number of things,
I'm sure we should all be as happy as kings.

ROBERT LOUIS STEVENSON, *Happy Thought*

Good-bye, proud world! I'm going home.
I am going to my own hearth-stone,
Bosomed in yon green hills alone,—
A spot that is sacred to thought and God.

EMERSON, *Good-Bye*

...now the world without leaving his own home.
LAO-TSZE, *The Simple Way*

The world is a beautiful book, but of little use to him who cannot read it.

CARLO GOLDONI, *Pamela nubile*

All is for the best in the best of possible worlds.
VOLTAIRE, *Candide*

This is a good world. We need not approve of all the items in it, nor of all the individuals in it; but the world itself, which is more than its parts or individuals, which has a soul, a spirit, a fundamental relation to each of us deeper than all other relations—is a friendly world.

JAN C. SMUTS

Toil and Life

It is work which gives flavor to life.
AMIEL, *Journal*

When your work speaks for itself, don't interrupt.
HENRY J. KAISER

The high prize of life, the crowning fortune of a man, is to be born with a bias to some pursuit which finds him in employment and happiness.

EMERSON, *Conduct of Life*

Great is work which lends dignity to man.
Babylonian Talmud

Man comes and tills the field and lies beneath,
And after many a summer dies the swan.

TENNYSON, *Tithonus*

Work is the inevitable condition of human life, the true source of human welfare.

TOLSTOY, *My Religion*

For he that is true of his tongue, and of his two hands,
And doth his work therewith, and willeth no man ill,
He is a god by the gospel.

WILLIAM LANGLAND, *Piers Plowman*

So every carpenter and workmaster, that laboureth night and day: and they that cut and grave seals, the smith also, sitting by the anvil, the potter sitting at his work,——all these trust to their hands: and every one is wise in his work.

Apocrypha: Ecclesiasticus, XXXVIII, 27-34

The labourer is worthy of his hire.

New Testament: Luke, X, 7

The only kind of labor which gives the workingman a title to all its fruits is that which he does as his own master.

POPE PIUS XI

In all labour there is profit.

Old Testament: Proverbs, XIV, 23

The Fruits of Labor

There is nothing truly valuable which can be purchased without pains and labour.

ADDISON, *The Tatler*

I believe that every right implies a responsibility; every opportunity, an obligation; every possession, a duty.

JOHN D. ROCKEFELLER, JR.

The deed is everything, the glory naught.

GOETHE, *Faust*, Part Two

Toil is the law of life and its best frui*
LEWIS MORRIS, *The Ode of l*

Say not the struggle nought availeth
ARTHUR

What is vulgar, and the essence of all vulgarity, but the avarice of reward? 'Tis the difference of artisan and artist, of talent and genius, of sinner and saint. The man whose eyes are nailed, not on the nature of his act, but on the wages, whether it be money, or office, or fame, is almost equally low.

EMERSON, *Conduct of Life*

The modest want of every day
The toil of every day supplied.
SAMUEL JOHNSON, *On the Death of Dr. Robert Levet*

Do what thy manhood bids thee do, from none but self
    expect applause;
He noblest lives and noblest dies who makes and keeps
    his self-made laws.

Sir RICHARD BURTON, *The Kasîdah*

Never is there either work without reward, nor reward without work being expended.

LIVY, *History*

A day's work is a day's work, neither more nor less, and the man who does it needs a day's sustenance, a night's repose, and the due leisure, whether he be painter or ploughman.
GEORGE BERNARD SHAW, *An Unsocial Socialist*

Experience, the Teacher

Experience seems to be like the shining of a bright lantern. It suddenly makes clear in the mind what was already there, perhaps, but dim.

WALTER DE LA MARE, *Come Hither*

All experience is an arch, to build upon.
HENRY ADAMS, *Education of Henry Adams*

By far the best proof is experience.
BACON, *Novum Organum*

Experience is a good school, but the fees are high.
HEINE

•erience inkreases our wizdum but don't reduse our phollys.
H. W. SHAW, (Josh Billings)

Experience is no more transferable in morals than in art.
        J. A. FROUDE, *Short Studies on Great Subjects*

> Experience, next, to thee I owe,
> Best guide; not following thee, I had remain'd
> In ignorance; thou open'st wisdom's way,
> And giv'st access, though secret she retire.
>   MILTON, *Paradise Lost*

> And others' follies teach us not,
>   Nor much their wisdom teaches;
> And most, of sterling worth, is what
>   Our own experience preaches.
>   TENNYSON, *Will Waterproof's Lyrical Monologue*

Experience: in that all our knowledge is founded; and from that it ultimately derives itself.
        JOHN LOCKE, *Essay Concerning Human Understanding*

I have but one lamp by which my feet are guided, and that is the lamp of experience.

        PATRICK HENRY

Experience cannot deliver to us necessary truths; truths completely demonstrated by reason. Its conclusions are particular, not universal.
        JOHN DEWEY, *The Quest for Certainty*

Men are wise in proportion not to their experience but to their capacity for experience.
        GEORGE BERNARD SHAW, *Maxims for Revolutionists*

Fame and Fortune

Money will buy money's worth; but the thing men call fame, what is it?

        CARLYLE, *Memoirs of the Life of Scott*

Fame is not popularity. It is the spirit of a man surviving himself in the minds and thoughts of other men.
        WILLIAM HAZLITT, *Lectures on the English Poets*

Fame is the spur that the clear spirit doth raise
(That last infirmity of noble mind)
To scorn delights, and live laborious days.
                              MILTON, *Lycidas*

There is this difference between renown and glory—the latter
depends upon the judgments of the many, the former on the
judgments of good men.
                              SENECA, *Epistulæ ad Lucilium*

Fame, like water, bears up the lighter things.
And lets the weighty sink.
                              CALDERÓN, *Adventures of Five Hours*

Upon the very books in which philosophers bid us scorn ambition, they inscribe their names. They seek publicity for
themselves on the very page where they pour contempt upon
publicity.
                              CICERO, *Pro Archia Poeta*

Herein the only road to fame and fortune lies:
Put not your trust in vinegar—molasses catches flies!
                              EUGENE FIELD

No true and permanent Fame can be founded except in labors
which promote the happiness of mankind.
                              CHARLES SUMNER, *Fame and Glory*

Sleep on, O brave-hearted, O wise man that kindled the
    flame—
To live in mankind is far more than to live in a name.
                              VACHEL LINDSAY, *The Eagle That is Forgotten*

The renown which riches or beauty confer is fleeting and
frail; mental excellence is a splendid and lasting possession.
                              SALLUST, *Catiline*

Immortal heirs of universal praise!
Whose honours with increase of ages grow,
As streams roll down, enlarging as they flow;
Nations unborn your mighty names shall sound,
And worlds applaud that must not yet be found.
                              POPE, *Essay on Criticism*

If a man knows the law, people find it out, tho' he live in a pine shanty, and resort to him. And if a man can pipe or sing, so as to wrap the prisoned soul in an elysium; or can paint landscape, and convey into oils and ochres all enchantments of Spring and Autumn; or can liberate and intoxicate all people who hear him with delicious songs and verses; it is certain that the secret cannot be kept: the first witness tells it to a second, and men go by fives and tens and fifties to his door.

EMERSON

The fortune which nobody sees makes a man happy and unenvied.

BACON, *Ornamenta Rationalia*

The day of fortune is like a harvest day,
We must be busy when the corn is ripe.

GOETHE, *Torquato Tasso*

The schemes of a hundred learned men are all inferior to one lone goddess, Fortune.

PLAUTUS, *Pseudolus*

A man is never so on trial as in the moment of excessive good-fortune.

LEW WALLACE, *Ben Hur*

The brave man carves out his fortune, and every man is the son of his own works.

CERVANTES, *Don Quixote*, Pt. II

Business and Commerce

A business, like an automobile, has to be driven, in order to get results.

B. C. FORBES

Keep thy shop, and thy shop will keep thee.

GEORGE CHAPMAN, *Eastward Hoe*

Drive thy business or it will drive thee.

BENJAMIN FRANKLIN, *Poor Richard's Almanac*

Never fear the want of business. A man who qualifies himself well for his calling, never fails of employment.

THOMAS JEFFERSON, *Writings*

A man at work at his trade is the equal of the most learned doctor.

HEBREW PROVERB

Good merchandise finds a ready buyer.

PLAUTUS, *Poenulus*

A man must have a certain amount of intelligent ignorance to get anywhere.

CHARLES F. KETTERING

A business with an income at its heels
Furnishes always oil for its own wheels.

COWPER, *Retirement*

Let your discourse with men of business be short and comprehensive.

GEORGE WASHINGTON

When a man's business does not fit him, 'tis as ofttimes with a shoe—if too big for the foot it will trip him, if too small, will chafe.

HORACE, *Epistles*

Business dispatched is business well done, but business hurried is business ill done.

BULWER-LYTTON

Cherish the little trade which thou hast learned, and be content therewith.

MARCUS AURELIUS, *Meditations*

Deeds are for Doing

Whatever is worth doing at all, is worth doing well.

LORD CHESTERFIELD, *Letters*

Whatsoever thy hand findeth to do, do it with thy might.
Old Testament: Ecclesiastes, IX, 10

As we are, so we do; and as we do, so it is done to us.
EMERSON, *Conduct of Life*

If you'd have it done, Go: if not, Send.
BENJAMIN FRANKLIN, *Poor Richard's Almanac*

Things won are done, joy's soul lies in the doing.
SHAKESPEARE, *Troilus and Cressida*

Great things are done when men and mountains meet;
This is not done by jostling in the street.
WILLIAM BLAKE, *Gnomic Verses*

Great deeds cannot die;
They with the sun and moon renew their light
For ever, blessing those that look on them.
TENNYSON, *The Princess*

I am monarch of all I survey.
WILLIAM COWPER, *The Solitude of Alexander Selkirk*

Do what thy manhood bids thee do, from none but self
expect applause.
SIR RICHARD BURTON, *The Kasîdah*

Our grand business undoubtedly is, not to see what lies dimly
at a distance, but to *do* what lies clearly at hand.
CARLYLE, *Essays: Signs of the Times*

Our deeds determine us, as much as we determine our deeds.
GEORGE ELIOT, *Adam Bede*

Man is of soul and body, formed for deeds
Of high resolve; on fancy's boldest wing.
SHELLEY, *Queen Mab*

All the beautiful sentiments in the world weigh less than a
single lovely action.
JAMES RUSSELL LOWELL, *Among My Books*

It is not book learning young men need, nor instruction about this and that, but a stiffening of the vertebrae which will cause them to be loyal to a trust, to act promptly, concentrate their energies, do a thing—"carry a message to Garcia."

ELBERT HUBBARD, *A Message to Garcia*

Serving One's Fellow Man

In order that you may please, you ought to be forgetful of self.

OVID, *Amores*

Serve and thou shalt be served. If you love and serve men, you cannot, by any hiding or stratagem, escape the remuneration.

EMERSON, *Lectures and Biographical Studies*

Small service is true service while it lasts:
Of humblest Friends, bright Creature! scorn not one:
The Daisy, by the shadow that it casts,
Protects the lingering dew-drop from the Sun.

WORDSWORTH, *To a Child*

Gratitude is one of those things that cannot be bought. It must be born with men, or else all the obligations in the world will not create it.

LORD HALIFAX, *Works*

The only persons I really care for are those who are of use to me.

NAPOLEON

A woman can forgive a man for the harm he does her, but she can never forgive him for the sacrifices he makes on her account.

SOMERSET MAUGHAM

The trivial round, the common task,
Would furnish all we ought to ask—
Room to deny ourselves; a road
To bring us, daily, nearer God.

JOHN KEBLE, *The Christian Year*

No personal consideration should stand in the way of performing a public duty.

ULYSSES S. GRANT

You must act in your friend's interest whether it pleases him or not; the object of love is to serve, not to win.

WOODROW WILSON

A Purpose in Life

The world turns aside to let any man pass who knows whither he is going.

DAVID STARR JORDAN

God, give me hills to climb,
And strength for climbing!*

ARTHUR GUITERMAN, *Hills*

Caesar, when he went first into Gaul, made no scruple to profess that he would rather be first in a village than second at Rome.

BACON, *The Advancement of Learning*

Though ambition itself be a vice, it is often the cause of great virtue. Give me that wit whom praise excites, glory puts on, or disgrace grieves; he is to be nourished with ambition, pricked forward with honour, checked with reprehension, and never to be suspected of sloth.

BEN JONSON

Hardly anything will bring a man's mind into full activity if ambition be wanting.

Sir HENRY TAYLOR, *The Statesman*

For mortal daring nothing is too high.
In our blind folly we storm heaven itself.

HORACE, *Odes*

* From *Death and General Putnam and 101 Other Poems* by Arthur Guiterman. Published and copyright, 1935, E. P. Dutton & Co., Inc., N. Y.

Ah, but a man's reach should exceed his grasp,
Or what's a heaven for?

BROWNING, *Andrea del Sarto*

Hitch your wagon to a star. Let us not fag in paltry works
which serve our pot and bag alone. Let us not lie and steal.
No god will help. We shall find all their teams going the other
way: every god will leave us. Work rather for those interests
which the divinities honor and promote,—justice, love, freedom, knowledge, utility.

EMERSON, *Society and Solitude*

A good man, through obscurest aspirations,
Has still an instinct of the one true way.

GOETHE, *Faust*

He rises on the toe: that spirit of his
In aspiration lifts him from the earth.

SHAKESPEARE, *Troilus and Cressida*

A lover of Jesus and of truth can lift himself above himself
in spirit.

THOMAS Á KEMPIS, *De Imitatione Christi*

Slight not what's near, through aiming at what's far.

EURIPIDES, *Rhesus*

He who would arrive at the appointed end must follow a
single road and not wander through many ways.

SENECA, *Epistulæ ad Lucilium*

To love the beautiful, to desire the good, to do the best.

MOTTO OF MOSES MENDELSSOHN

Bread, Money, and Taxes

Cast thy bread upon the waters: for thou shalt find it after
many days.

Old Testament: Ecclesiastes, XI, 1

Half a loaf is better than no bread.
                    JOHN HEYWOOD, *Proverbs*

Back of the loaf is the snowy flour,
And back of the flour the mill,
And back of the mill is the wheat and the shower
And the sun and the Father's will.
MALTBIE D. BABCOCK, *Give Us This Day Our Daily Bread*

If you would know the value of money, go and try to borrow some.
                    BENJAMIN FRANKLIN, *Poor Richard's Almanac*

When it is a question of money, everybody is of the same religion.
                    VOLTAIRE

Money, th' only power
That all mankind falls down before.
                    SAMUEL BUTLER, *Hudibras*

Blessed is the man who has both mind and money, for he employs the latter well.
                    MENANDER, *Demioyplos*

Money, says the proverb, makes money.
                    ADAM SMITH, *Wealth of Nations*

It is easy at any moment to resign the possession of a great fortune; to acquire it is difficult and arduous.
                    LIVY, *History*

For the love of money is the root of all evil: which while some coveted after, they have erred from the faith, and pierced themselves through with many sorrows.
                    New Testament: I Timothy, VI, 10

Money never made any man rich, but his mind. He that can order himself to the law of nature, is not only without the sense, but the fear of poverty.
                    BEN JONSON

FRIENDSHIP

Choosing Companions

Tell me what company thou keepest, and I'll tell thee what thou art.

CERVANTES, *Don Quixote*

Who can enjoy alone,
Or all enjoying, what contentment find?
JOHN MILTON, *Paradise Lost*

No man can be provident of his time that is not prudent in the choice of his company.

JEREMY TAYLOR, *Holy Living and Dying*

A man's mind is known by the company it keeps.
JAMES RUSSELL LOWELL, *My Study Windows: Pope*

How universally God joineth like to like!
MENANDER, *The Man from Sicyon: Fragment*

The more closely you associate yourself with the good, the better.

PLAUTUS, *Aulularia*

Good company upon the road, says the proverb, is the shortest cut.

OLIVER GOLDSMITH, *Vicar of Wakefield*

The most agreeable of all companions is a simple, frank man, without any high pretensions to an oppressive greatness; one who loves life, and understands the use of it; obliging alike at all hours; above all, of a golden temper and steadfast as an anchor. For such an one we gladly exchange the greatest genius, the most brilliant wit, the profoundest thinker.

LESSING

I never found the companion that was so companionable as solitude.

HENRY DAVID THOREAU, *Walden*

A True Friend

A faithful friend is the medicine of life.
Apocrypha: Ecclesiasticus, VI, 16

A friend is a person with whom I may be sincere.
EMERSON, *Essays*

One friend in a lifetime is much; two are many; three are hardly possible.
HENRY ADAMS, *Education of Henry Adams*

Greater love hath no man than this, that a man lay down his life for his friends.
New Testament: John, XV, 13

Be slow in choosing a friend, slower in changing.
BENJAMIN FRANKLIN, *Poor Richard's Almanac*

What is thine is mine, and all mine is thine.
PLAUTUS, *Trinummus*

A good man is the best friend, and therefore soonest to be chosen, longer to be retained; and indeed, never to be parted with.
JEREMY TAYLOR, *A Discourse of the Nature, Measures, and Offices of Friendship*

No receipt openeth the heart but a true friend.
BACON, *Essays: Of Friendship*

A true friend unbosoms freely, advises justly, assists readily, adventures boldly, takes all patiently, defends courageously, and continues a friend unchangeably.
WILLIAM PENN, *Fruits of Solitude*

To have the greatest blessing, a true friend.
PHILIP MASSINGER, *Parliament of Love*

They are rich who have true friends.
THOMAS FULLER, *Gnomologia*

Those friends thou hast, and their adoption tried,
Grapple them to thy soul with hoops of steel;
But do not dull thy palm with entertainment
Of each new-hatch'd, unfledged comrade.
SHAKESPEARE, *Hamlet*

A man that hath friends must shew himself friendly: and
there is a friend that sticketh closer than a brother.
Old Testament: Proverbs, XVIII, 24

He will never have true friends who is afraid of making
enemies.
HAZLITT, *Characteristics*

For friendship, of itself a holy tie,
Is made more sacred by adversity.
DRYDEN, *Hind and the Panther*

A friend in need is a friend indeed.
RICHARD GRAVES, *The Spiritual Quixote*

Be courteous to all, but intimate with few, and let those few be
well tried before you give them your confidence. True friendship is a plant of slow growth, and must undergo and with-
stand the shocks of adversity before it is entitled to the
appellation.
WASHINGTON, *Letter*, 1783

He does good to himself who does good to his friend.
ERASMUS, *Familiar Colloquies*

Gifts and Giving

A gift is as a precious stone in the eyes of him that hath it.
Old Testament: Proverbs, XVII, 8

Give, and it shall be given unto you; good measure, pressed
down, and shaken together, and running over.
New Testament: Luke, VI, 38

The wise man does not lay up treasure. The more he gives to others, the more he has for his own.

LAO-TSZE, *The Simple Way*

If thou doest aught good, do it quickly. For what is done quickly will be acceptable. Favors slowly granted are unfavorably received.

AUSONIUS, *Epigrams*

Rings and jewels are not gifts, but apologies for gifts. The only gift is a portion of thyself. . . . Therefore the poet brings his poem; the shepherd, his lamb; the farmer, corn; the miner, a gem; the sailor, coral and shells; the painter, his picture; the girl, a handkerchief of her own sewing.

EMERSON, *Essays*

Behold, I do not give lectures or a little charity,
When I give I give myself.

WALT WHITMAN, *Song of Myself*

If thou hast abundance, give alms accordingly; if thou hast but a little, be not afraid to give according to that little.

Apocrypha: Tobit, IV, 8

If of thy mortal goods thou art bereft,
And from thy slender store two loaves alone to thee are left,
Sell one, and with the dole
Buy hyacinths to feed thy soul.

SAADI

We must take care to indulge only in such generosity as will help our friends and hurt no one; for nothing is generous, if it is not at the same time just.

CICERO, *De Officiis*

My purse, my person, my extremest means
Lie all unlock'd to your occasions.

SHAKESPEARE, *The Merchant of Venice*

To receive a present handsomely and in a right spirit, even when you have none to give in return, is to give one in return.

LEIGH HUNT, *The Seer*

Good Neighbors

There is an idea abroad among moral people that they should make their neighbours good. One person I have to make good: myself. But my duty to my neighbour is much more nearly expressed by saying that I have to make him happy—if I may.
ROBERT LOUIS STEVENSON, *A Christmas Sermon*

A bad neighbor is as great a plague as a good one is a blessing; he who enjoys a good neighbor has a precious possession.
HESIOD, *Works and Days*

To act against one another is contrary to nature; and it is acting against one another to be vexed and to turn away.
MARCUS AURELIUS, *Meditations*

Wouldst thou have men speak good of thee? Speak good of them. And when thou hast learned to speak good of them, try to do good unto them, and thus thou wilt reap in return their speaking good of thee.
EPICTETUS, *Golden Sayings*

No man is an island entire of itself; every man is part of the main. If a clod be washed away by the sea, Europe is the less, as well as if a promontory were, as well as if a manor of thy friends or thine own were. Any man's death diminishes me because I am involved in mankind, and therefore never send to know for whom the bell tolls; it tolls for thee.
JOHN DONNE, *Devotions Upon Emergent Occasions*

Thou shalt love thy neighbour as thyself.
Old Testament: Leviticus, XIX, 18

Your own safety is at stake when your neighbor's house is in flames.
HORACE, *Epistles*

Good fences make good neighbors.
ROBERT FROST, *Mending Wall*

The honor of a neighbor should be held as sacred as one's own.
Hebrew Proverb

In the field of world policy I would dedicate this nation to the policy of the good neighbor.

F. D. ROOSEVELT (from his Inaugural address, 1933)

For Friendship's Sake

Friendship is a word the very sight of which in print makes the heart warm.

AUGUSTINE BIRRELL, *Obiter Dicta*

Friendship is nothing else than an accord in all things, human and divine, conjoined with mutual good-will and affection.

CICERO, *De Amicitia*

Without confidence there is no friendship.

EPICURUS

Fame is the scentless sunflower, with gaudy crown of gold;
But friendship is the breathing rose, with sweets in every fold.

OLIVER WENDELL HOLMES, *No Time Like the Old Time*

Friendship is a union of spirits, a marriage of hearts, and the bond thereof virtue.

WILLIAM PENN, *Fruits of Solitude*

Nothing is meritorious but virtue and friendship, and, indeed, friendship is only a part of virtue.

ALEXANDER POPE

Great souls by instinct to each other turn,
Demand alliance, and in friendship burn.

JOSEPH ADDISON, *The Campaign*

If a man does not make new acquaintances, as he advances through life, he will soon find himself left alone. A man, Sir, should keep his friendship in constant repair.

SAMUEL JOHNSON, (Boswell's *Life*)

The perfect friendship is that between good men, alike in their virtue.

ARISTOTLE, *Nicomachean Ethics*

Gratitude

While I would fain have some tincture of all the virtues, there is no quality I would rather have, and be thought to have, than gratitude. For it is not only the greatest virtue, but even the mother of all the rest.

CICERO, *Pro Plancio*

Gratitude is the memory of the heart.

JEAN BAPTISTE MASSIEU, *Letter to the Abbé Sicard*

Gratitude is a nice touch of beauty added last of all to the countenance, giving a classic beauty, an angelic loveliness, to the character.

THEODORE PARKER, *Sermon: Of Moral Dangers
Incident to Prosperity*

Let never day nor night unhallow'd pass,
But still remember what the Lord hath done.

SHAKESPEARE, *II Henry VI*

One good turn deserves another

PETRONIUS, *Satyricon*

In everything give thanks.

New Testament: 1 Thessalonians, v, 18

Sweet is the breath of vernal shower,
The bee's collected treasures sweet,
Sweet music's melting fall, but sweeter yet
The still small voice of gratitude.

THOMAS GRAY, *Ode for Music*

No metaphysician ever felt the deficiency of language so much as the grateful.

C. C. COLTON, *Lacon*

Gratitude preserves auld friendships and begets new.

Scottish Proverb

Man and Society

Man was formed for society.
WILLIAM BLACKSTONE, *Of the Nature of Laws in General*

When a man meets his fitting mate society begins.
EMERSON, *Uncollected Lectures: Social Aims*

The spirit of truth and the spirit of freedom—they are the pillars of society.
HENRIK IBSEN, *Pillars of Society*

Society, saith the text, is the happiness of life.
SHAKESPEARE, *Love's Labour's Lost*

Life is action and passion; therefore, it is required of a man that he should share the passion and action of his time at peril of being judged not to have lived.
JUSTICE OLIVER WENDELL HOLMES

Society waits unform'd, and is for a while between
    things ended and things begun.
WALT WHITMAN, *Thoughts: Of These Years*

Without society, and a society to our taste, men are never contented.
JEFFERSON, *Writings*

Society is now one polish'd horde,
Form'd of two mighty tribes, the bores and bored.
LORD BYRON, *Don Juan*

Oh to the club, the scene of savage joys,
The school of coarse good-fellowship and noise.
COWPER, *Conversation*

My business in the social system is to be agreeable; I take it that everybody's business in the social system is to be agreeable.
DICKENS, *Bleak House*

Heart for Heart

The heart of the wise, like a mirror, should reflect all objects, without being sullied by any.

CONFUCIUS, *Analects*

The heart hath its own memory, like the mind,
    And in it are enshrined
The precious keepsakes, into which is wrought
    The giver's loving thought.

LONGFELLOW, *From My Arm-Chair*

The heart ay's the part ay
    That makes us right or wrang.

ROBERT BURNS, *Epistle to Davie*

Where your treasure is, there will your heart be also.

New Testament: Luke, XII, 34; *Matthew* VI, 21

My heart is ever at your service.

SHAKESPEARE, *Timon of Athens*

He that is of a merry heart hath a continual feast.

Old Testament: Proverbs, XV, 15

To thee only God granted
A heart ever new:
To all always open,
To all always true.

MATTHEW ARNOLD, *Parting*

Her heart is always doing lovely things,
    Filling my wintry mind with simple flowers;
Playing sweet tunes on my untuned strings,
    Delighting all my undelightful hours.

JOHN MASEFIELD, *Her Heart*

Kind hearts are more than coronets,
    And simple faith than Norman blood.

TENNYSON, *Lady Clara Vere de Vere*

I account more strength in a true heart than in a walled city.
                                              JOHN LYLY, *Endymion*

> In sailing o'er life's ocean wide,
> Your heart should be your only guide;
> With summer sea and favouring wind
> Yourself in port you'll surely find.
>   W. S. GILBERT, *Ruddigore*

The heart has its reasons, which reason does not know.
                                              PASCAL, *Pensées*

> I do not hunger for a well-stored mind,
> I only wish to live my life, and find
> My heart in unison with all mankind.
>   EDMUND GOSSE, *Lying in the Grass*

On Giving and Taking Advice

When all is done, the help of good counsel is that which
setteth business straight.
                              BACON, *Essays: Of Friendship*

Let the counsel of thine own heart stand: for there is no man
more faithful unto thee than it. For a man's mind is some-
time wont to tell him more than seven watchmen, that sit
above in an high tower.
                Apocrypha: Ecclesiasticus, XXXVII, 13, 14

No gift is more precious than good advice.
                              ERASMUS, *Convivium Religiosum*

It is awfully easy to be hard-boiled about everything in the
daytime, but at night it is another thing.
                         ERNEST HEMINGWAY, *The Sun Also Rises*

He that won't be counselled can't be helped.
                BENJAMIN FRANKLIN, *Poor Richard's Almanac*

Whatever advice you give, be brief.
                                              HORACE, *Ars Poetica*

There is often as much good sense required in knowing how
to profit from good advice as there is to give it.

LA ROCHEFOUCAULD, *Maximes*

He who counsels, aids.

PLAUTUS, *Curculio*

Share the advice betwixt you: if both gain, all
The gift doth stretch itself as 'tis receiv'd,
And is enough for both.

SHAKESPEARE, *All's Well that Ends Well*

In giving advice, seek to help, not to please, your friend.

SOLON

He is the best of all men who follows good advice.

ZENO

Brotherhood

"Men work together," I told him from the heart,
"Whether they work together or apart."

ROBERT FROST, *The Tuft of Flowers*

Of a truth, men are mystically united: a mysterious bond of
brotherhood makes all men one.

THOMAS CARLYLE, *Essays: Goethe's Works*

I think, am sure, a brother's love exceeds
All the world's loves in its unworldliness.

ROBERT BROWNING, *A Blot in the 'Scutcheon*

Let brotherly love continue.

New Testament: Hebrews, XIII, 1

Down in their hearts, wise men know this truth: the only
way to help yourself is to help others.

ELBERT HUBBARD, *The Philistine*

Heav'n forming each on other to depend,
A master, or a servant, or a friend,
Bids each on other for assistance call,
Till one man's weakness grows the strength of all.

ALEXANDER POPE, *Essay on Man*

No one can be perfectly free till all are free; no one can be perfectly moral till all are moral; no one can be perfectly happy till all are happy.

HERBERT SPENCER, *Social Statics*

Lo, soul! seest thou not God's purpose from the first?
The earth to be spann'd, connected by network,
The people to become brothers and sisters,
The races, neighbors, to marry and be given in marriage,
The oceans to be cross'd, the distant brought near,
The lands to be welded together.

WALT WHITMAN, *Passage to India*

Index

(All page numbers refer to the page on which the quotation commences. The author's name will appear on the following page if the passage carries over.)

N

Napoleon I, (Bonaparte), 39, 214
Nash, Ogden, 147
Nathan, George Jean, 135
Nesbit, Edith, 147
New Testament, see Bible, The
Noüy, Lecomte du, 37
Noyes, Alfred, 126

O

Old English Rhyme, 197
Old Testament, see Bible, The
O'Malley, Austin, 202
O'Neill, Eugene, 52
Overstreet, Harry A., 106, 128
Ovid, 48, 134, 158, 186, 190, 214

P

Page, William Tyler, 57
Paine, Thomas, 37, 71, 92, 171
Palladas, 104
Parker, Dorothy, 92
Parker, Theodore, 64, 225
Parton, James, 68
Pascal, Blaise, 130, 178, 200, 228
Payne, John Howard, 75
Peattie, Donald Culross, 140
Penn, William, 220, 224
Percival, James Gates, 152
Perry, Commodore Oliver Hazard, 71
Peterson, Houston, 178
Peterson, Roger Tory, 152
Petit-Senn, Jean-Antoine, 200
Petrarch, 151
Petronius, 225
Phaedrus, 182
Phillips, Wendell, 92
Pittacus, 103
Plato, 15, 50, 51, 120, 169, 171
Plautus, 95, 194, 211, 212, 219, 220, 229
Pliny the Younger, 165
Plutarch, 105, 168
Poe, Edgar Allan, 15, 85, 121
Poling, Daniel A., 33

Pope, Alexander, 42, 44, 48, 81, 93, 94, 97, 99, 124, 132, 134, 144, 170, 178, 186, 210, 224, 230
Pope Benedict XV, 36
Pope Pius XI, 207
Porter, Noah, 188
Post, Emily, 97
Pound, Ezra, 120
Powys, John Cowper, 100, 104
Powys, Llewelyn, 121
Procter, Bryan Waller, 186
Propertius, Sextus Aurelius, 24
Proverbs,
  Arab, 116
  English, 194
  French, 24, 107, 131
  Greek, 96
  Hebrew, 212, 223
  Hindu, 51
  Old, 196
  Scottish, 225
  Spanish, 87
  Turkish, 96
Putnam, Israel, 71

Q

Quintilian, 94

R

Rabelais, François, 95, 130, 131, 196
Raleigh, Sir Walter, 41, 94
Rank, Otto, 131
Ravensworth, Lord, 158
Ray, John, 28, 30, 75, 81, 106
Reade, Charles, 18
Renan, Ernest, 199
Rhys, Ernest, 132
Richter, Jean Paul, 26, 45
Riley, James Whitcomb, 141
Rivarol, Antoine de, 198
Robespierre, Isidore Maximilien de, 176
Robinson, Edwin Arlington, 70
Roche, James Jeffrey, 174
Rockefeller, John D., Jr., 207
Rogers, Will, 130, 193

Roosevelt, Franklin Delano, 72, 107, 173, 177, 179, 224,

Roosevelt, Theodore, 58, 124

Root, George Frederick, 63

Rosenwald, Julius, 199

Rossetti, Christina Georgina, 86, 151

Rossetti, Dante Gabriel, 161

Rostand, Edmond, 28

Rousseau, Jean-Jacques, 87, 95

Roux, Joseph, 157

Runyon, Damon, 201

Ruskin, John, 83, 93, 112, 116, 154

Russell, Bertrand, 102, 108, 129, 184

Russell, George W. (AE), 15

Russell, George William Erskine, 185

S

Saadi, 222

Saint Augustine, 102, 123

Saint Francis de Sales, 95

Saint Thomas Aquinas, 118

Sallust, 210

Sand, George, 108

Sandburg, Carl, 15, 125, 132

Santayana, George, 34, 50, 72, 99, 123, 203

Sappho, 21, 24, 81, 161

Saunders, Frederick, 132

Savile, George, see Halifax, Lord

Schiller, Friedrich von, 78, 128, 143

Schumann, Robert, 112

Schwartz, Jean, see Jerome, William

Schweitzer, Albert, 101, 113

Scott, Sir Walter, 25, 143, 156, 190

Sears, Edmund Hamilton, 166

Seeger, Alan, 106, 128

Selden, John, 198

Seneca, 91, 106, 123, 182, 189, 210, 216

Seward, William Henry, 34

Shakespeare, William, 15, 17, 19, 22, 23, 24, 27, 29, 30, 39, 42, 44, 52, 79, 86, 89, 91, 94,

95, 102, 113, 122, 125, 135, 136, 140, 144, 146, 150, 155, 160, 163, 166, 175, 183, 184, 185, 190, 191, 194, 197, 198, 199, 205, 213, 216, 221, 222, 225, 226, 227, 229

Shaw, David T., and Becket, Thomas A., 58

Shaw, Frances, 76

Shaw, George Bernard, 37, 148, 203, 208, 209

Shaw, Henry Wheeler, (Josh Billings), 200, 208

Shelley, Percy Bysshe, 24, 41, 77, 121, 126, 142, 150, 155, 159, 213

Sheridan, Richard Brinsley, 106, 139

Sidney, Sir Henry, 196

Sidney, Sir Philip, 163

Silver, Rabbi Abba Hillel, 37

Smith, Adam, 217

Smith, Alexander, 182

Smith, Captain John, 72

Smith, Logan Pearsall, 105, 203

Smith, Sydney, 181

Smuts, Jan Christiaan, 206

Sockman, Ralph W., 172

Socrates, 50, 51

Solon, 100, 131, 229

Sophocles, 23, 79

Southey, Robert, 148, 171, 195

Spalding, Albert, 127

Spencer, Herbert, 230

Spenser, Edmund, 45, 98, 141, 147, 190

Spinoza, 53

Spock, Dr. Benjamin M., 83

Staël, Madame de, 27

Stanley, Arthur Penrhyn, 18

Stanton, Colonel Charles E., 72

Stanton, Edwin McMasters, 70

Starrett, Vincent, 117

Steele, Richard, 79, 86, 111, 170

Stefferud, Alfred, 153

Stendhal, (Henri Beyle), 199

Stephens, James, 203

Sterne, Laurence, 194

Stevenson, Adlai E., 59